Christmas
Miracles

Christmas Miracles

MAGICAL TRUE STORIES
OF MODERN-DAY MIRACLES

Jamie C. Miller, Laura Lewis, and
Jennifer Basye Sander

WILLIAM MORROW AND COMPANY, INC.

NEW YORK

Library of Congress Cataloging-in-Publication Data

Christmas miracles : magical true stories of modern-day miracles /
Jamie C. Miller, Laura Lewis, and Jennifer Basye Sander
p. cm.
ISBN 0-688-15588-X
1. Miracles. 2. Christmas. 3. Religious biography. I. Miller, Jamie C.
II. Lewis, Laura, 1963–   . III. Sander, Jennifer Basye, 1958–   .
BT97.2.C455 1997
242'.335—dc21   97-15524
                                                                          CIP

Printed in the United States of America
First Edition
1 2 3 4 5 6 7 8 9 10
BOOK DESIGN BY JO ANNE METSCH

To Julian, Evan, Olivia, Alex, Ian, Kelly, Seth, and Ryan

Our own miracles

C O N T E N T S

Contents

Contents

Each day comes bearing its gifts. Untie the ribbons. . . .

—Ann Ruth Schabacker

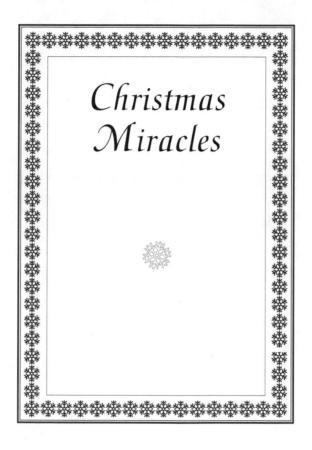

Christmas
Miracles

INTRODUCTION

miracle n. 1. An event that seems impossible to explain by natural laws and so is regarded as supernatural in origin or as an act of God. 2. One that excites admiration or awe.
— Webster's II New Riverside Dictionary

EACH YEAR AT Christmas even the most jaded hearts are softened by reports of wondrous occurrences, from unlikely reunions to dramatic medical recoveries, from newly formed romances to the sudden reappearance of long-lost possessions. Why should these things happen then, and why do we feel so touched by them?

During the Christmas season all people the world over are looking for miracles, opening their hearts to the possibility of a miracle for just a few short weeks. World-weary souls soften and become open windows through which miraculous deeds can fly and happen upon the unwary, who might shut them out at other times of the year. Churchgoers sit amid hundreds of flickering candles at midnight services, remembering an ancient pilgrimage to a stable and a star, awed by the beauty of the sight and ready to see an angel on the road that night. Tired shoppers drag home from yet another crowded mall, disheartened by the season's commercialism and willing to see a miracle in the small gesture of a stranger. Miracles big and small happen every day during Christmastime—if we are open and receptive to them.

In the pages of *Christmas Miracles* you will find true stories of miraculous occurrences that happened to folks just like you: small, sweet stories of remarkable events that happened on or near Christmas. You will read of those who are suddenly willing to stoop down and consider the needs or desires of little children; people who remember the weaknesses and loneliness of the elderly; folks who, if only for one short season, stop asking how much their friends love them and instead wonder how much love they can show to their friends.

We three editors all come from families with strong storytelling traditions, and no night is a better night for stories than Christmas Eve. After the dinner dishes were cleared away and the small children sent up to bed, we listened late into the night as our parents and grandparents told old family stories like that of the young doctor's all-night walk home alone through the countryside on Christmas night after saving the life of a farm boy, the father's payment of a dozen fresh eggs carefully cradled in his black medical bag, or the Swedish folktale about the bear who saves the life of a wealthy landowner, only to lose his own life in return. And so one night when we found ourselves sharing these stories together, we realized that there must be a wider audience for these true tales of Christmas miracles. May you and your family enjoy each story and may you bask in their glow for the year to come.

Albert Einstein said, "There are only two ways to live your

life. One is as though nothing is a miracle. The other is as if everything is." It is our hope that the stories in *Christmas Miracles* weave the magic of brotherhood, fill hearts with peace, and cause a frightened world to pause—to remember—and to hope. As you read these stories, keep your eyes open, keep your heart open, and let the miracles begin.

Christmas Loaves
and Fishes

O N CHRISTMAS EVE in homes everywhere, there is quiet excitement. The festive feeling and the warmth of having family near brings to mind a Christmas tale I love to relate each year. It's a true story, even though it might sound unbelievable. And it gives proof that miracles do happen.

A long time ago there was a group of young people who decided to spread some Christmas cheer. They had discovered that there were several children who would be spending the festive day in a community hospital nearby. So they bought nice presents, wrapped them and, armed with guitars, sweet voices and one of the friends dressed as Santa Claus, dropped in unexpectedly at the hospital on Christmas Eve.

The children were overjoyed at seeing Santa, and by the time the group was finished handing out presents and singing Christmas carols, there were tears in everyone's eyes. From then on, it was decided they would play Santa every year.

The following Christmas Eve, the ladies at the hospital were included in the rounds, and by the third year it was expanded to embrace some poor children in the neighborhood.

On the fourth Christmas Eve, however, after all the rounds were made, Santa Claus looked into his bag and discovered there were a few extra toys left. So the friends mulled it over, trying to figure out what to do with them. Somebody mentioned that there were a few squatters' shacks nearby in which a couple of desperately poor families lived.

So the group decided to go there, thinking there were perhaps three families at most. But as they drove over the crest of the hill into this lonely area—it was around midnight now—the shocked group saw a large number of people standing at the side of the street.

They were children—more than thirty of them. Behind them were not three shacks but rows and rows of shabby squatters' dwellings. As the cars drew to a stop, the children came running up, shouting with joy. It turned out they had been waiting patiently all night for Santa Claus. Somebody—no one could remember who—had told them he was coming, although *our* Santa had decided to go there only moments before.

Everyone was stunned, except for Santa. He was in a panic. He knew he didn't have enough toys for all these kids. Eventually, not wanting to disappoint the children, he decided to give whatever toys he had only to the smallest children. When the presents ran out, he'd just have to explain to the bigger kids what had happened.

So moments later he found himself perched on top of a

car's hood as these thirty or more sparkling clean children, dressed in their best clothes, lined up in order of height, with the smallest first, for their moment with him. As each anxious child approached, Santa dipped into his bag, his heart heavy with dread, hoping to find at least one more toy. And, by some miracle, he found one each time he dipped. And as the last of the children received a present, Santa looked into the now deflated bag. It was empty— empty as it should have been twenty-four children ago.

With relief, he let out a hearty "Ho ho ho" and bade the kids farewell. But as he was about to enter the car (the reindeer, apparently, had the day off), he heard a child scream, "Santa! Santa! Wait!" And out of the bushes rushed two little children, a boy and a girl. They had been asleep.

Santa's heart sank. This time he knew for sure he had no more toys. The bag was empty. But as the out-of-breath kids approached, he summoned up some courage and dipped into the bag once more. And, lo and behold, there were two more presents in there.

The group of friends, now all grown adults, still talk about this miracle on Christmas morning. They still have no explanation for it, other than the fact that it happened. How do I know so much about this? Well, I was the one playing Santa.

—RAYNIER MAHARAJ
Toronto, Canada

Christmas Saved
My Mother's Life

ANY STUDENT OF the twentieth century would affirm that the Holocaust was one of the darkest chapters of modern history. Yet within that nightmare, there were moments of humanity and life-giving compassion.

In August of 1942 my mother, Fania Paszt, was one of the last survivors of the Lutsk ghetto in Poland. She was a young girl, not yet twenty years old, when her life was saved by the miraculous appearance of one righteous Christian after another. No one could ever know why she was spared and her parents, her brothers, and other family members were so brutally murdered. Evangelical Christians, farmers and peasants each arrived at a precise life-saving moment to hide her in attics, cellars, and chicken coops.

My mother's Christmas miracle began on August 19, 1942, when a Ukrainian peasant came into the ghetto and proposed a plan to hide my mother's family in the town.

Not wanting to jeopardize her entire family with a risky plan, my mother tore off the yellow Star of David patch that she was required to display as a Jew, covered her head with a shawl, and, leaving behind her entire family, set out with the peasant to test the escape route. Luck was with them, and she was able to slip out from the ghetto without being stopped by the unusually large number of Ukrainian police and German soldiers gathered on its edges. The plan was to return the next morning and smuggle her entire family out with her. However, as she approached the ghetto the next day, she was stopped by a Ukrainian policeman. Taking her for a fellow Christian, not a Jew, he warned her away from the area. "It has been sealed off for official reasons."

Jews had lived in Lutsk since the tenth century and had flourished with the city as it became a political and economic center in the mid-sixteenth century. But on the morning of August 20, the day my mother stood outside the ghetto, an order had been given to end that history once and for all. Over the course of the next two days, seventeen thousand Jews from the Lutsk ghetto were led to the Polanka Hill on the outskirts of the city, thrown live into pits, and machine-gunned to death. Every Jew found within the borders of the ghetto was murdered.

My mother's brave expedition out of the ghetto had saved her. Having lost everything and everyone, my dazed mother returned to her guide's home and spent the next few months hidden in the flue of his outdoor country oven.

But on December 24, 1942, Fania Paszt's luck seemed to run out. The Ukrainian peasant who had saved her life feared for his own safety should he continue to harbor her, and turned her out of his house. My mother wandered the dirt roads of the countryside, freezing cold in her tattered cotton dress. As night descended, she knew her life was at its end. Recognizing the manor house of the county warden, she turned up its path. The warden's dogs jumped on her, ripped her dress, and bit her. The warden, hearing the commotion of the dogs, appeared at his door with a gun in his hand.

"Please shoot me," my mother begged. "Let me share the fate of my family." "I cannot kill you tonight," responded the official. He took her inside, fed her some of his own family's Christmas Eve dinner, and gave her a new dress and a place to sleep for the night. The next morning, fearful that he could be killed for saving a Jew, he took her into town and gave her over to another Christian family to hide. Three more Christians magically stepped forward during the war to save her life until the day she descended from an attic during the Russian liberation of Lutsk in 1944. She was one of the few Jews still alive in the town.

Only decades later did I learn of the Polish expression, "On Christmas Eve, even a stray cat is allowed to live." On the evening of December 24, 1942, my mother had been like a stray cat in the Polish countryside. At that precise moment, God had to invoke Christmas Eve to save her life. I am proud of my Jewish heritage and of my calling as a rabbi, but I will never forget the legacy that Christmas saved my mother's life. "Merry Christmas to all," from a grateful rabbi.

—RABBI ABIE INGBER
Cincinnati, Ohio

The Stranger

I T WAS CHRISTMAS EVE twenty years ago, the very first Christmas we spent in our small, red wooden farmhouse on the outskirts of a forest in the north of Sweden. The place was old and very old-fashioned but so cheap that we could afford it. It had a small stable where we could keep a few horses and two small fields for the horses to run in. A narrow road led out to the main road. We were so far from the closest town that ours was always one of the last roads to be cleared of snow.

This Christmas seemed magical to us. Our family had never lived in the country before. Snow had been falling for days and the whole world was white and soft with downy snow. The neighborhood looked like a frozen sea with giant white frozen waves. Late on that day, the snow stopped falling and the clouds vanished slowly. Pale sunshine from the sinking sun was reflected in sparkling cascades on the snow.

The birches and pine trees in the forest were furry with snow.

It was like living in one of those glittering Christmas cards, and we were childishly happy in the silent whiteness. This winter seemed like a special gift made exclusively for us. Along with my husband and our two young children, I felt that this was a Christmas when anything could happen.

We had our traditional Christmas dinner late in the day, gathered around our old kitchen table. It was a traditional Swedish holiday dinner—a big ham, ribs, cabbage, and peas, served with breads, cheeses, and sausages of all kinds. Afterward we sat talking together in the flickering candlelight in the small sitting room and ignored the piles of dirty dishes in the kitchen.

Just then—at half past ten on a pitch-dark Christmas night—someone pounded on our front door.

We looked at each other around the table. We did not yet know any of our new neighbors, and of our old friends, who could possibly be dropping in on us, given that we lived so far from town? Another knock sounded. I got up and went to see who it was.

There in the snow, quite alone and with a sparkling, star-studded sky shining behind him, stood a complete stranger. On this cold Swedish night he wore no hat. His soft blond hair formed a halo around his head, his breath grew like a cloud out of his half-open mouth, and a pair of big eyes shone in a very pale face.

I stared at him. Then I looked out into the yard beyond him to see if anyone was with him. The yard was empty.

All I could see was the deep, black holes in the snow that marked his path up to the front door.

He just stood there as I looked at him, his hands in his pockets, watching me. At last he spoke.

"Excuse me, ma'am, but have you got a television set?"

His question was so unexpected that I did not quite know what to say.

"Ah, well, yes . . . yes we have," I said.

"Could you possibly let me watch a television program? I think there is one I'd like to see." His voice was soft and friendly. I stood silent. My first thought was that I must say no in the politest way possible. But although my mind thought of refusal, my tongue refused to say no. Deep inside I seemed to hear the voice of my pious old grandfather telling me, "The Christmas night is holy. You must never turn anyone away from your house that night, for if you do you are turning away Christ."

"Well . . ." I said slowly, trying to think of what to do. "What program would that be?"

"I don't remember," he said, "but if you will let me look in the newspaper I will tell you which one."

"Maybe you had better come in," I said, and opened the door the rest of the way.

The young man walked up the three steps and held out his hand for a firm handshake. He did not say what his name was and I did not ask. His hand was icy cold and I quickly saw the reason why: He had no mittens on. He was dressed in a worn gray trench coat buttoned up to his chin and he wore big rubber boots. Not much to wear on a cold winter night, I said to myself.

His eyes were blue like the summer sky, and when he smiled, I was surprised to see the trust in his eyes and on his face. I got the distinct feeling that he had been certain that I would let him in.

I invited him into the warm kitchen. As he stepped into the room, he caught sight of the food still spread on the table.

"Oh," he said quietly. "You have eaten, I see."

I was surprised to hear myself say, "Maybe you would like to taste some Christmas food?" By then my husband and children had joined us in the kitchen. None of them asked for an explanation of the stranger's presence. I had let him in and that was enough for them. The blond man smiled at them and shook their hands, still calm and trusting as a kitten.

Then he turned to the wood fire range and rubbed his hands together to warm them, glancing over at the dinner table while he stood there. "Yes," he said, in answer to my question. "If you have enough food, it would be very nice."

I relit the candles while the stranger walked around the table looking into the bowls and pots. He seemed unfamiliar with most of the dishes, and when he came to the red cabbage, he stopped and his eyes grew wide.

"But what is this?" he exclaimed. "It is quite black! Is there *blood* in it?"

"No," I assured him. "Red cabbage always turns black when you cook it in an iron pot."

"How strange," he muttered. "Perhaps I won't eat it."

Ham and bread, green cabbage and Christmas sausage,

spareribs and peas, he tasted everything slowly and with a look of great concentration.

My little daughter stood close to me, staring quietly while he ate. At last our Christmas guest got up, thanking me for the feast. "If I may borrow the newspaper, I would like to check on the television programs." He got it and started reading while my daughter's eyes followed him, round and thoughtful. "Let's see, how about this show here?"

I looked over his shoulder at the TV guide. "It is too late for that one; was that the one you wanted to see?"

"I do not know," he said. "But this one, look! I am sure that this one is good. I would very much like to see it." He stepped into the little room where our television stood, pulled a chair from near the wall, and planted himself in front of the set. "Now then," he said. "How do you switch this on?"

His words sounded a bit solemn and his strange blue eyes were as eager as a child's, a child expecting a glorious treat.

We switched the set on for him and the whole family sat down to join him. A comedy was just starting, a funny story of the kind that the whole family can watch, even very young children. The stranger did not look at us while the television was on. He followed the story closely, and when the action grew frantic, he threw his head back and laughed so that his angel's hair flew around him.

The film had a happy ending. My husband reached over and snapped off the set. The night was silent outside the house. The stranger was still laughing quietly to himself. "Just imagine," he said softly. "Today I have even laughed."

He turned in his chair and looked at us, still with laughter in his cheeks. He looked carefully at each one of us as if he wanted to remember our faces. We all sat silently for a few minutes.

"Where are you going?" my husband asked.

"To Copenhagen," was his answer. "I come from the north of Sweden and I am going there to save people. There is so much sin there and the people need help."

"How do you travel?" my husband asked again. "By car?"

"No. I walk."

Had he walked the 700 or 800 miles from the north of Sweden to our house in the woods? And was he planning to walk the hundreds of miles south to Denmark as well?

The words hung in the air. The stranger smiled and laughed once again with his strange and carefree tone. "Sometimes kind people give me a ride, sometimes I walk, sometimes I get food, and tonight I have even laughed." His blue eyes twinkled in genuine joy as if he had been given a grand gift.

He and my husband went on talking about this and that for a little while as I sat wondering what to do with our strange guest.

Our daughter pulled at my skirt and whispered, "Mum, is he going to spend the night here?"

I shook my head, quite at a loss. It was the stranger himself who solved the problem. Suddenly he got up and announced that he really must be going.

"Are you really going to . . . walk?" I asked. "There are no people on the roads tonight and the next town is far away."

"I'll be fine," he said, calmly.

He had this strange smile. It was not polite, not embarrassed. It broke out spontaneously as if he could not hold it back, an eager smile. It seemed as if he were looking forward to something we did not know or as if he had seen something we could not see.

Without thinking, I took a big orange from the fruit bowl and handed it to him. "Here, at least you will have something to eat while you are walking."

His smile broke out again. He took the orange and held it in his hand like a king holding his orb. "Imagine," he said reverently. "This orange has traveled all the way around the world to Sweden and now I am holding it in my hand. Is that not fantastic?"

Suddenly we all saw the orange with his eyes—a fantastic ripe orange from a warm country far, far away—and we too marveled at the sight.

He put the orange into his pocket. His hands were warm when he shook ours.

The Christmas night was absolutely still, cold and clear. The moonlight poured down over the sparkling whiteness and the lonely stranger, who took big steps in the deep snow. His footprints looked like black holes and his shining blond hair was the last we saw of him as he disappeared between the trees on his way back to the main road.

We watched him quietly, and then turned to go back into our warm house. It was my daughter who spoke first.

"Was that Jesus?" she asked.

I smiled an adult's smile. "No, it was not. You know, it is a very long time since Jesus was born on Christmas."

"I know!" she said impatiently. "But he can come whenever he wants to, can't he? I think that was Jesus!"

The next morning, on Christmas Day, we tried to follow the stranger's deep footprints toward the main road. But suddenly, we had to stop. Right there, in the middle of our own little path out to the road, the footprints suddenly ceased. We looked all around us at the pure untouched snow. No footprints, no car tire marks, absolutely nothing.

When we came to know our neighbors in the following months we always asked if they had seen a stranger walking alone on the road that Christmas night. No one had seen any sign of a stranger.

We never learned who the stranger was, or how he disappeared. But we cannot help wondering. . . .

—KERSTIN BACKMAN
Grängesberg, Sweden

O Christmas Tree

CHRISTMAS 1990 FOUND our family in a new home in California, due to my husband's job transfer. We missed the beautiful snow-covered mountains of our Utah home; the weepy drizzle and fog of our new location felt strange and depressing during the holiday season. We longed for the traditions of a white Christmas complete with sledding, snowmen in our front yard, and playful snowball fights with our four young daughters. Cozy holiday get-togethers with Grandma, aunts, uncles, and cousins were now replaced with cordial neighborhood parties given by well-meaning but nevertheless unfamiliar new acquaintances. But we were determined to "bloom where we were planted" and we tried to remain cheerful in spite of feeling dreadfully homesick.

We had hoped to make the six-hundred-mile trek back to see our families sometime during the holiday, but the economy had taken a nose-dive that year and our budget wouldn't allow any unnecessary extravagance. At least we had a nice new home, which was cheerfully decked from floor to ceiling with ornaments, ribbons, boughs, and lights we had collected over the years. And then there was our tree. It stood in the big bay window of our living room and was covered with all the beautiful glass ornaments I had so carefully wrapped months before, not wanting to lose a single one during our move. Our house was located on the corner of a well-traveled street and I knew the tree looked radiant to all those who drove by.

The evening of December 12 our girls were begging to sleep under the tree in their sleeping bags as we often did as a family, reading Christmas stories and munching on goodies. Although I had sometimes allowed this tradition even on school nights in December, my practical side took over and I reminded them that there would be plenty of nights for this after school closed for the holidays. A little disgruntled and teasing me that I had turned into a "Scrooge," they finally settled down for the night, two girls in each bedroom.

About 2:00 A.M. we were suddenly shocked out of our sleep by a loud crash followed instantly by the deafening scream of our burglar alarm. My husband, Greg, leaped from our bed and, being a Vietnam vet, instinctively grabbed his gun, yelling at me to call 911. Knowing I wouldn't be able to communicate over the shriek of the alarm, I punched in the code numbers to turn it off. Then I called for help. When the 911 operator asked the nature of the emergency, I hysterically responded that I didn't know except that our house had been broken into, setting off our alarm. Almost at the same moment, I heard Greg yelling that our house had been hit by a car! The operator asked for our address. Firemen were on their way. We invited a very drunk driver into our house to call his parents, and he was taken away in handcuffs by the police moments later. Neighbors gathered in pajamas and robes, shaking their heads in disbelief and offering words of comfort. A capable crew of public servants worked for hours to clean up the debris, scooping our treasures like trash out into the yard. Plastic sheets were put up in an effort to contain our house and protect it from the elements for the few remaining hours before daylight.

Morning came and, yes, our nightmare was a reality. Assessing the damage in the light of day was shocking: The car had come right through our bay window and knocked down the whole front wall along with the window. Of course, our tree, along with many other precious possessions, was demolished. As we scrounged through the heaps of trash, looking for anything to salvage, we noticed a houseplant that had been across the room from the Christmas tree, with a perfect round hole in one of its large leaves. On closer examination, we discovered a small round ornament sitting unbroken in the dirt. The ornament had shot through the leaf with such violent force that it had punched a hole through the leaf in its exact shape. Although we had lost many beautiful things in the accident, we were suddenly aware of the deadly impact of the crash, and were humbly grateful that our four little blond girls had not been sleeping under the tree, as they had so desperately wanted to do the night before. As their mother, I knew in my heart I had been prompted to be uncompromising in my insistence that they sleep in their own rooms that night. We were heartsick over our losses, but we were becoming vaguely aware of the miracles that were just beginning.

As the details of the night unfolded, we learned that our girls had acted heroically. In one room, our daughter Gretchen had instructed her younger sister to hurry into the closet. In the other bedroom, Lauryn had told her younger sister to get under the bed. Even in their own terror, their thoughts were for each other's safety. The emotional damage, however, took longer to heal than the physical damage. It would be weeks before the girls would feel secure in their own beds. They, too, realized how easily someone could have been seriously injured.

Driving through our neighborhood that morning, a building contractor named Steve Larsen noticed the mess and, wondering how a tornado had struck only one house on the block, stopped to offer his help. He became our dear friend over the next few weeks and was able to work miracles in getting our house repaired in fairly short order. Considering how slowly the gears of the legal system turned, and our complicated insurance policies, this process could have taken months to get going, but Steve's compassionate efforts resulted in the rebuilding beginning that very day. He was even able to acquire a new bay window for us from a manufacturer who had a month-long waiting list. I remember one of his subcontractors confiding in us that, although he was very sorry for our situation, he was also thankful for the work. He hadn't worked many months and this job meant that his family would be able to have a Christmas.

Our phone rang constantly with offers of help. "Do you need meals brought in while you are trying to clean up? . . . Are you warm enough? . . . Do you need heaters? . . . Should we organize some men from the neighborhood to watch your house until it is secure so you can sleep at night?" Neighbors who previously had given only a nod or an obligatory wave now stopped to introduce themselves, expressing their concern and leaving their phone numbers in case we needed anything. Unfamiliar joggers and walkers who had previously seen happy girls playing in the front yard now stopped to inquire about our daughters, expressing relief that no one had been injured or killed. We began to feel the arms of love that would hold us up over the next several months.

The night of the church Christmas party was fast approaching, and although Greg and I certainly weren't in a partying mood and were exhausted from all the cleanup, we decided that the girls needed to attend *something* normal and festive during the holidays. When everyone at the party started singing carols, I choked back tears, feeling like I couldn't remain cheerful or positive one more minute, in light of the incredibly stressful week we had just experienced. When the evening was finally over, we came home, glad to roll our tired bodies into bed for a few precious hours of sleep. Just at that moment, we suddenly heard people singing outside—carolers on the front porch. My heart sank. I just knew I couldn't force one more smile for a group of jubilant people, much less open the door to reveal my disheveled house.

But it was too late. One of the girls quickly opened the

door and we stood there in our pajamas, listening to thirty or forty familiar voices sing "O Christmas Tree, O Christmas Tree, how lovely *were* your branches!" The song continued with words specially created for our circumstances, from friends with eyes full of caring and love. I don't remember the words to the song as much as I remember our feelings, as small wrapped packages started being passed over the heads of the carolers and into our arms. We each took several in our hands and had to put them down to receive the rest. We were instructed to "open *before* Christmas" and then the group excused themselves, as the hour was late.

We stared in wonder at the pile of gifts. As we gathered in a circle and began to unwrap each one, our hearts were full as we saw before us scores of new ornaments for a future tree: beautiful glass icicles, angels, a blown-glass heart, a bit of felt on which "JOY" had been stitched in sequins, a delicate silver nativity. One creative couple with a sense of humor had hammered a matchbox car and attached a hook to it; it took its rightful place among the more elegant ornaments. Handmade, store-bought, each ornament was a token of love and an effort to "bear ye one another's burdens . . ." (Gal. 6:2). New priceless treasures from new cherished friends. We were indeed loved.

Christmas 1996 found the Gardner family somewhat melancholy as we watched the drippy drizzle from the Utah skies. Another job transfer had replanted us back in our beautiful snow-covered mountains, and although we were happy to be with old friends and family, we longed for our

California friends. For, in five short years, through good times and bad, we had grown to love another "family" in a place we could truly call "home."

—JANNIS GARDNER
Sandy, Utah

Chester

CHESTER FIRST CAME into our family with a tough assignment: win over five people who didn't want him. He had the unenviable task of replacing Coots, our lovable tiger cat, who had just died of feline leukemia. My father, brother, two younger sisters, and I were so heartbroken over the loss of Coots that we decided it was best not to have a pet for a while—so we were all shocked the early December afternoon when my mother came home with a tiny black-and-white fur ball with pink paws in her arms.

Chester Festus Aldo Emery was the name we eventually settled on, and he took the job of winning us over very seriously. By Christmas, after he'd only been with us a few weeks and was still tiny and fragile, he would sneak out of his bed in the middle of the night, scale the stairs, nestle himself on my pillow, and purr contentedly.

As the months and years passed, Chester's unique quirks

continually endeared him to me—quirks such as walking around the rim of the bathtub whenever I took a bath, hiding in empty paper bags, hopping onto the Lazy Susan whenever it was opened, and wanting to perch himself on my shoulders when I walked through the house. But the most peculiar thing about him was his love for playing fetch with a minature nylon flag. The ratty, hole-filled white flag with the blue words FAIRBANKS MUSEUM was stapled to a small black stick. At precisely six-thirty every night, as I sat doing homework or watching TV, Chester would enter my room with the flag between his teeth and drop it at my feet. I'd throw it down the stairs, and like a dog he'd bound after it. I'd hear the quick patter of his paws going down, then up, and within seconds he'd be back, whiskers twitching, tail wagging, purring like a racecar and raring to do it again. This would go on for about twenty-five throws per session or until I'd finally had enough—he could have gone on indefinitely.

Chester was a house cat, and never seemed interested in going outdoors, but sometimes he lingered just a little too close to the door for my liking. Whenever someone knocked on the door, or the door was opened, the refrain "Make sure the cat doesn't get out!" could be heard through the house, and it was me doing the talking. Just to make sure, I'd usually rush to the door to be certain that Chester was safe.

The day after Thanksgiving, during my senior year in high school, I had just thrown the flag down the stairs for the first time that night when I heard a light tap at the front door. Before I had a chance to look down the stairwell, the door had been opened. It was our neighbor, Charlie Williams, a close friend of the family who was in the habit of opening the door before we could get to it. Charlie's heavy boot entered the hall and landed squarely on Chester's tail. A high-pitched yowl followed and before my foot hit the top stair, Chester was out the door.

We finally quit searching after three hours. Calling his name in the darkness did no good. There was no sign of the flag, no sign of anything. In three years, Chester had never been out, and his survival prospects weren't that good—especially with a Doberman and a German shepherd in the neighborhood, both of which ran free, and the fact that we lived at the corner of the busiest traffic intersection in town.

I was up before dawn, out looking again. Nothing. No traces, which was good, I figured; at least he wasn't in the road. I went door to door in the neighborhood; we posted signs, called the radio station, took out newspaper ads, everything. Nothing at all materialized. It was as though Chester had vanished into thin air. I went out onto the front porch every night calling his name while my brother and sisters cried behind me.

As the days passed, it was hard to get through a day of school without the tears welling up, especially after ten inches of snow fell. Winter was settling in to northeast Vermont, and with it the grim reality that I'd never see Chester again.

I had trouble sleeping at night because I missed his warm circle on my pillow and his licking my face in the morning. Finally, a few days before Christmas, my parents told me I should stop calling for Chester because it was bothering the other kids too much.

On a very sad Christmas Eve, as we were getting ready to go to bed, we got a frantic call from our neighbor Charlie, the friend who had accidentally let Chester out that night in November. A water pipe had burst in his basement and he needed help fixing it. My father, an excellent handyman, got some tools together and he and I headed over to help out next door.

Charlie's cellar was a mess. Water was spraying in all directions, soaking piles of laundry, wood, family mementos, everything. "Thank goodness we didn't hide the children's Christmas presents down here!" Charlie said, as he surveyed the chaos. My father soon found the source of the leak and we began to patch it up. After about half an hour it was repaired well enough to hold for a few days. From the stairwell, we looked around the basement one more time.

In a far corner, sticking out from behind a covered woodpile, a soiled, white piece of nylon caught my eye. "Wait a minute, Dad!" I said, and I moved toward it, slowly at first, and then very quickly. In the faint light I reached down and picked it up. My eyes flooded with tears when I realized it was Chester's flag. I crouched down and shone my flashlight into the crack behind the pile. Two feet in, looking back at me, were two cloudy, barely open cat eyes in a head that no longer had the strength to move. I yelled out and both Charlie and my father rushed back down the stairs. We carefully moved the wood off the pile to get to Chester.

"He must have fallen through the cellar window and been too scared to meow," Charlie said. "He's probably been down here the whole month. I covered the cellar windows with plastic on the last Saturday in November."

Frail and thin, Chester wasn't far from death. I gently picked him up. His eyes closed with relief. He was breathing, but just barely. As I carried him up the stairs, I placed the flag on his stomach and could hear the faint sound of purring and feel the muscles in his tail futilely attempting to wag.

Miraculously, after a visit to the vet and several weeks of tender loving care, Chester pulled through and returned to his old sprightly self. He lived with our family for many happy years after that. What might have been one of our saddest family holidays became instead one of our most memorable, and now, almost fifteen years later, I still place that tattered old flag on the Christmas tree every year in honor of Chester.

—JOHN EMERY
Clifton Park, New York

One Last Wish

OUR CHRISTMAS MIRACLE started early that year—in January, to be exact. That was symbolic in many ways. The first of the year—a new beginning—a starting-over place. Expectations, hopes, dreams, and goals. A perfect time for miracles.

I've heard it said that there are no small miracles. And ours would not be small. We would learn important lessons of life that would change us in ways still hard for us to comprehend. We had struggled through so many losses the previous year. The loss of our family business, personal finances, our family home, and more important, our dreams. Yes, that year left us humble and meager, but the struggle made us stronger and wiser.

We were excited to start a new year. Never had we possessed so little and believed so much. Nineteen ninety-four—that was to be our year. A year of rebuilding, healing, and recovery. However, nothing we dreamed of or planned could have prepared us for the events that would soon take place.

It was cold and dark on that special night in January when my husband, Cal, first heard it. We had just started a new business and Cal was working alone in one of his back offices. He suddenly heard the voice of a small girl calling out, "Daddy . . . Daddy . . . Daddy." Thinking that a little girl had gotten lost, he searched the outside reception area, and even the parking lot. Finding no one, he returned to his office to finish his work. Then he heard the girl's voice again: "Daddy . . . Daddy . . . Daddy." Because he was alone in the office, Cal tried to come up with a logical explanation. When he came home that night, he told me about his experience. He seemed bewildered, and yet neither of us could find any answers, and so with a family to care for, we turned our attention to other responsibilities.

It was only a few days later on a peaceful, quiet afternoon at home when she came. Cal was watching a sporting event on television downstairs; I was upstairs trying to catch up on a project. I suddenly heard the sound of Cal's footsteps running up the stairs and I could hear the heaviness of his breath even before he found me. White as a sheet and shaking, he reached out for me. His words tumbled over each other in his haste to tell me what had happened. He had been sitting in his chair watching the game on TV when he heard again the voice of a small girl calling out. It was a clear voice, very close and soft. "Daddy, Daddy, Daddy." Cal quickly turned his head toward the voice and saw a small girl standing just a few feet away from his chair, looking directly into his eyes. He jumped out of the chair and turned again to find her gone. Then he ran up the stairs to find me.

Now this was something we couldn't explain away or simply dismiss from our minds. What could it mean? Why had this happened? Was God trying to tell us something, and if so, what? Could this be our child? It didn't make any sense. We had a total of eight children between us: four of them married, a daughter at college, and three boys at home. After having three boys in a row, could this be the daughter I had dreamed of and longed for? But why now, so late in our lives? I couldn't fathom it and jokingly replied, "Honey, maybe she meant to say 'Grandpa,' but it was too big a word for such a little girl." Yet as I prayed that night, I asked for answers: Was a daughter to come to our family? At our age? With eight other children? What of our finances, or lack of them? And then, as I had become accustomed to doing, I concluded with a simple "Thy will be done."

It came as no surprise when, a few weeks later, I found I was carrying a baby. Knowing it was to be a girl, I rushed to the fabric store and came home with arms full of pink fabric. I sewed blankets, dresses, comforters, and crib sets, all in pink! I sewed my way through the summer and into fall. Cal was working hard to develop his clientele for his new business in addition to working as a sales manager for a dealership. By November, he was feeling exhausted and I was very overdue. But as if the year had not produced enough incredible experiences already, we were in for yet another surprise.

Cal had been saying he had a stomachache for a few

weeks. Because he rarely complained, although he had experienced pain most of his life due to a birth defect, I was concerned. I thought perhaps he had an ulcer from all the stress of the past two years, and so he went in for some routine tests. Shortly after he returned from having some X rays taken, his doctor called us at home. "Mrs. Stewart," she said, "I need to see you and your husband in my office in one hour." I was immediately overcome with a feeling of despair.

The air in the doctor's office was thick and heavy. I was very uncomfortable, being twenty-one days overdue, and Cal struggled quietly with his own pain. The doctor's words came quickly and were straight to the point: "Mr. and Mrs. Stewart, I am sorry to tell you that Cal has cancer. It seems to have started in your esophagus, but it has spread to your liver, stomach, and lymph nodes. It is terminal. I hope you will live to see the birth of your child."

For a minute I thought I was losing my mind. I could hardly believe I had heard the doctor say she hoped Cal would live to see the birth of his child. Couldn't she see I was due to deliver at any moment? I felt my head spinning as I tried to listen to what she was saying and keep myself from crying. We stumbled from her office to the car. I don't know how we got home. I do remember being at the foot of our bed that afternoon, holding hands as Cal offered up to God the desires of his heart, asking for a healing, a blessing. He cried. I had been with him for so many years, decades almost, and could only remember him crying two times before.

Over the next few days we went from doctor to doctor

and tried to make plans. Cal had decided he was not going to die from cancer. Other people had survived such a thing, so why not Cal?

Just three days after his diagnosis, on November 19, our daughter was born. Little Rebecca created quite a stir as she made her entrance into the world that night. What a wonderful event it was! The room was full of family, children, and friends. During the whole ordeal, I felt Cal at my side, his arm around my shoulder and his hand on my arm. My support, my strength, as he had always been. I didn't notice then how sick he had become that day. And it wouldn't be until Christmas that he would tell me about the other touching events of that evening. He said that he had felt fine during the whole night, until the moment Rebecca was born. As he touched her little body as she lay on my chest and as he realized she was all right, he began to feel himself slipping away. He struggled for a chair and quietly fought the feeling of death that had overcome him at the very moment life had entered his newborn baby.

In the wee hours of the morning, Cal, on bended knees, pleaded for his life. Humbly and with faith, he begged for more time. Not for himself—he now knew it was his time to go—but for his children, his wife. How could he leave her on the night she had just given birth? Who would take care of her, or the other children? "Please, please," he begged, "for my wife, my children, please give me more time. Please just give me Christmas."

It was dawn before he struggled up from his knees and fell into bed. God would grant him his last wish.

And so on Christmas we celebrated. We celebrated life,

family, the blessings God had given us. We celebrated the birth of His Son, Jesus Christ, and the birth of our perfect little daughter. Family and friends came from across the country to be with us on Cal's last Christmas. It was a joyous time as we felt the love of so many around us.

And then Christmas was over—the carolers were gone from our doorstep, family and friends returned to their homes, the tree and the lights were taken down, and Cal's body ceased to struggle against the disease.

We slept with him in the hospital those last nights— Rebecca and I on a cot by his bed; another daughter, Rachel, in a chair. The cancer had spread to his brain, and he no longer could talk or see, or even stay awake. But for two days I watched in awe as another miracle unfolded. As each of his eight children came to say good-bye to their father— their hero—Cal would wake up, sit up in his bed, and listen to each child, and then share his love and tender feelings with each one.

The last day we were alone together. I crawled up into the hospital bed with him and tried to express the feelings of my heart. I felt so helpless without him—he had always taken care of me, of all of us. I talked to him for hours, reminding him of all the love and laughter we had shared, the dreams, the wonderful experiences of our life together. I thanked him for teaching me by his great example to love, to trust, to give. I thanked him for each of our beautiful children, for his strength, his patience, his forgiving heart. And I thanked him for waiting—for enduring his own pain to give us that last wonderful Christmas together.

And then I let him go. I assured him that the children

and I would be all right. He could go now to his heavenly home.

The little girl who had come to visit her "Daddy" almost a year before would now be the angel that would hold our family together through our extraordinary grief. Day by day, little Rebecca brought such joy and love to our broken hearts that we were able to begin healing. Cal had not only lasted through Christmas; he had given our family the greatest of all gifts—a part of himself that would last a lifetime.

—CYNTHIA STEWART-COPIER
Roseville, California

In memory of Calvin Eugene Stewart

Bologna from Heaven

Y GRANDMOTHER WAS not the "home-baked cookies and crocheted blankies grandma" sort at all.

She had lived the majority of her life as a widow with two children, working hard as a professional in a world unaccustomed to such things. A southern lady of appreciable means, she had hired help when my mother and my aunt were being raised, giving her distance from the day-to-day chores of child rearing. She was formal, aloof, almost Victorian—and utterly undomestic. From my earliest days I called her "Grandmother," so that you could practically hear the capital "G."

She certainly didn't know what to do with her first grandchild, a girl, who came to Winder, Georgia, for week-long summer visits. Grandmother's life was utterly adult, from the hard-edged brocade furniture and untouchable baby grand piano in her living room to her habit of living in solitary peace, eating most meals out. The presence of grandchildren had a way of complicating the routine.

Breakfast was easy enough: cereal. And we could always go out for dinner. But lunch was trickier—while she often skipped it herself, this was not an option for a growing young child. For the brief duration of those summer visits, she did the best she could to overcome her lack of culinary interest and skill.

Fried bologna sandwiches were the answer. At noontime while she cooked, I would sit on the white enameled table next to the stove, its smooth surface cool under my summer-tanned legs, my feet dangling off the edge. The slap of distant screen doors slamming and the squeals of neighbors' grandchildren playing in the midday heat poured in through the open window behind me.

I loved the ritual of preparing the sandwiches as much as the food itself. My job was to carefully peel away the red rubbery shell from each piece of bologna. Grandmother would put it into a hot, heavy cast-iron skillet, cooking only one slice at a time. I watched intently for the best part to happen—when heat made the bologna puff up in the center to resemble a pink bathing cap, with great force Grandmother would deflate the little cap with two businesslike whacks with the edge of a metal spatula, making a little cross in the center of the slice. Soon after that special step, the bologna was flipped over, and when the edges began to curl up from the heat, it was done. Placed on toasted white bread liberally slathered with Hellmann's mayonnaise, it was my lunch every day in Winder, Georgia.

As an adult I rarely eat meat at all, much less a highly

processed product of such questionable origin and ingredients as bologna. The sylvan days of hot Georgia summers are a long time away from my life today.

Grandmother had died the year I was married. Soon divorced, in dire financial straits from my former husband's shenanigans, and estranged from the rest of my family, I found myself living in a small, low-budget apartment shared with a roommate. Struggling to finish my college education on small student loans and slow-to-arrive grants, I was faced with a poor and lonely Christmas.

The contrast between my own plain life and the artificial gaiety that decorated the town was depressing. Christmas lights and silver tinsel hung from lampposts; huge winking stars decorated the intersections. My apartment was not decorated at all—I had no Christmas tree, no honey-baked ham, no tin of home-baked cookies on my table. The only bright spot in my life that year was my two little Pekingese dogs, Sandy and Samantha. They loved me unconditionally and were a tremendous source of comfort during those rough years.

Alas, not only did I have no tree, no ham, and no cookies, but I also had no dog food. No dog food and no money in my checking account. My next student loan payment was not scheduled to arrive for another week or so, and as the nursery rhyme says, my cupboards were bare. Now I could have made it for a week on my own without food, casually dropping in on friends near dinnertime or swallowing my pride and visiting a soup kitchen for a hot meal. But how could I feed my "girls"? Studying the figures in my checkbook, unable to find a forgotten dollar or a calculating mistake, I realized that the only way I could feed my little family was to write a check at the store while knowing full well that it would not be covered until my student loan arrived. I was horrified that this was the level to which I had sunk, sick at heart to think that I was about to resort to a life of crime, and depressed that there was no one to whom I could turn, no one to comfort me.

I screwed up my resolve and decided to "buy" only the most minimal essentials, not wanting to take advantage of the grocery store any more than I had to. No steak or lobster for me, just the basics. I wrote grocery list after grocery list, paring the items down to where I had but a few things that the dogs and I could not do without.

It was a long car ride to the local market. I entered with a heavy heart and slowly walked the aisles to find the few things on my list. Dog food, bread, milk, Top Ramen. Standing in line at the checkout counter, I was certain that everyone around me could sense what I was about to do. Christmas carols played over the sound system as I fidgeted. Finally it was my turn at the register. Blinking through tears of shame, I wrote out the check and handed it to the checkout girl. "Thank you. Have a merry Christmas," she said. I grabbed my bag and ran for the car.

I wept the whole way back to the apartment. What was my life coming to? Would I ever finish school, and would I ever get back on track financially?

Once home and unpacking my plunder, I reached into the sack for the last few items when my hand found an unfamiliar plastic package, cool to the touch. Puzzled, I pulled it out.

Bologna from Heaven

It was a five-pound package of Oscar Meyer bologna.

Bologna? That wasn't on my list! I hadn't eaten it in years, and I knew full well I hadn't put it into my cart at the store; it was way too expensive for me to "afford." I checked the receipt—the bologna wasn't there.

And then it hit me. Grandmother. She was trying to take care of me. From across the heavens she'd felt my hunger, my fear, and my despair, and she had reached out through the mists to comfort and care for me the only way she'd ever known how—with fried bologna sandwiches. Hours before, I'd been at the brink of starvation; now I had enough bologna and bread to eat until the next check arrived.

Crying again but this time from joy, I reached for a frying pan and set about making the best Christmas dinner I'd ever had. Every year since then I make fried bologna sandwiches on Christmas Eve, thwacking the puffed-up slices with the side of my spatula and remembering an extraordinary woman from Winder, Georgia.

—NORA LYNN
Sacramento, California

The Town That
Gave Christmas

I T WAS CHRISTMAS EVE, 1927, in the remote prairie town of Hillspring, Alberta, Canada. Mary Thomas Jeppson was getting her six small children ready for bed. She thought her heart would break as she watched five of her children dance around the small house, excited to hang their socks for Santa to fill. Her oldest daughter, Ellen, sat subdued and sullen in a corner of the cold, two-room house. Ellen's heart was heavy for a ten-year-old, but she understood the reality of what tomorrow would bring. She felt that her mother was cruel to let the children get their hopes up when she knew very well there would be nothing to fill the socks. They would be lucky to have a little mush for breakfast, as there was only a small amount of wheat and corn left. The winter had just started and already it was cold and harsh. The milk cow had died the week before from starvation and severe weather conditions, and the last two or three chickens had stopped laying eggs about a month before.

Mary helped each one of the children hang a little darned and mended sock. She tried to persuade Ellen to hang one, too, but Ellen just sat there, shaking her head and mumbling "Mom, don't do this. Don't pretend." After the socks had been hung, Mary read the Christmas story from the Bible and then recited a few Christmas poems from memory—and memories of her own happy childhood living in the United States flooded her mind. She was the next to youngest of a very large and loving family. Although they'd been pioneers in a remote area of Idaho, her mother and father had made life—and especially Christmas—very exciting and memorable.

Before Ellen went to bed, she pleaded with her mother to tell the children the truth. Mary kissed her daughter good night and whispered, "I can't, Ellen. Don't ask me why—I just can't tell them." It was almost midnight and the other children had been asleep for hours, and Mary's husband Leland had gone to bed, too, feeling like a broken man, like he had failed his family completely. Mary sat by the fire reading the Christmas story from the Bible over and over again. Her mind drifted to her plight here in this godforsaken land of ice and snow. It was the beginning of the Depression and her husband had heard wondrous stories about the unlimited opportunities of homesteading in Canada. After two years of not being able to find work in the United States and after a flood had destroyed their small home in Willard, Utah, he had decided to move his family to Canada. It seemed, however, that they were five or six years too late to cash in on the rumored opportunities. After several seasons of unusual weather conditions, most of their crops had frozen or failed.

In October Mary had received a letter from her family back in Idaho, asking what they could do to help and what they could send the family for Christmas. Mary had put off her response—she had too much pride to let them know how destitute her family really was. Finally in November, realizing that things were not going to get any better, she had written. She only mentioned the necessities: She told them how desperately they needed food, especially wheat, yeast, flour, and cornmeal. She related how long it had been since she had been able to bake a cake or cookies, because they had no molasses or honey, and of course, no sugar. It had been a year since they had had any salt to use on their food. She also added that it would be wonderful if they could ship just a little bit of coal, because of the cold, and because their fuel supply was almost depleted. She finished her letter with a request for some old, used quilts. All of hers had worn thin and were full of holes, and it was difficult keeping the children warm. She mentioned their need for anything to keep them warm—any used socks, shoes or gloves, warm hats or coats. And at the very end of the letter she wrote, "If you could just find a dress that someone has outgrown that I could make over to fit Ellen, please send that, too. Ellen is such a little old lady for such a young girl. She carries the worries of the whole family on her thin shoulders. She has only one dress that she wears all the time, and it is patched and faded. She has outgrown it, and I would like so very much to fix up something that is nicer for her."

The week before Christmas, Leland hitched up the horse and sleigh and made the three-hour round trip from Hill-spring into the town of Cardston every day to check at the train station and post office whether a package had come from their family in Idaho. Each day, he received the same disappointing answer. Finally, on the day before Christmas, he went into Cardston first thing in the morning and eagerly waited for the mail delivery. He left in the early afternoon to get home before dark and he left empty-handed. He wept openly as he rode home, knowing he would have to explain to Mary that perhaps the package would arrive the day after Christmas or the next week, but that it had not made it in time for the big day.

Mary suddenly awoke from her reminiscent sleep with a chill. The old clock on the wall said it was 3:30 A.M. The fire in the stove was all but out and she decided to add a little more fuel so that it wouldn't take so long to start in the morning. She looked over at the little limp socks still hanging by the fireplace and felt a similar emptiness in her heart. Outside, the wind was blowing at about seventy miles per hour—the snowstorm had intensified. Mary was about to put out the lantern and go to bed for a few short hours, when she heard a quiet knock at the door. Mary opened the door to find a man standing there, and in all her life she had never seen anyone look more like her vision of Santa Claus. He was covered with ice and snow and had a long beard, made white from the snow. His hat, his gloves, and boots were also white, and for a moment Mary thought she was dreaming.

It was the mailman, Mr. Scow from Cardston, who had

known the plight of the Jeppson family. He told her that he knew they had been waiting for packages from Idaho and he knew there would be no Christmas without them. That evening, as he was finishing up a long day of delivering mail all around the town, he was glad to be going home. His horse was exhausted and frozen as that day there had been one of the worst blizzards of the year. He was relieved to put his horse in the barn, park his sleigh, and return to the warmth of Christmas Eve at home with his family. But just as he was leaving, someone from the train station came running up to him and told him that ten large crates had just arrived from the States for the Jeppson family. It was only about four in the afternoon, but already it was dark and the storm was getting worse. They both decided there was nothing they could do about delivering the crates that night, but that they would be sure the Jeppsons received them the day after Christmas.

The mailman told Mary that when he went home, he had a disturbing feeling, and after discussing it with his wife, they decided that he needed to deliver the crates that night. He would have to find someone who would let him borrow a fresh horse and a sleigh with sharp running blades. After he finished telling Mary about his decision to come, he brought the crates into the house. She insisted that he thaw out and warm up by the stove while she went out to check on his horse. When she looked at the poor animal with icicles hanging from its nose and mouth, she knew it would never make the trip back to Cardston that night and she tried to talk Mr. Scow into staying until morning. He refused the offer, telling her that it had taken him almost eight hours to make the trip to her house in the storm, and if he were to leave now, he would still be able to spend Christmas afternoon with his family. So Mary told him she would harness their own horse, which was in better condition, to make the trip back. She got him some dry clothes, fed him what warm food she could muster, and he headed off to town. It was almost 5:00 A.M. and he probably wouldn't get home until around noon. Mary had thanked him as best she could, but for her whole life she maintained that there would never be sufficient words to express her gratitude. "After all," she would say, "how do you thank someone for a miracle . . . and a Christmas miracle at that?"

As soon as he left, Mary began to unpack the crates. She only had an hour or so before the children would awaken. At the top of one of the crates she found a letter from her sisters. As she began to read the incredible account, tears streamed down her face. They told her that quilting bees had been held all over the Malad Valley, and from these, six thick, warm, beautiful quilts were included. They told her of the many women who had sewn shirts for the boys and dresses for the girls, and of others who had knitted the warm gloves and hats. The donation of socks and shoes had come from people from miles around. The local church had even held a bazaar to raise the money to buy new coats and scarves for the whole family. All of the sisters, nieces and cousins, aunts and uncles had gathered to bake the breads and make the candy. There was even a crate half full of beef that had been cured and packed so that it could be shipped, along with two or three slabs of bacon and two hams. At the close of the letter, her sisters said, "We hope you have a merry Christmas, and thank you so much for making our Christmas the best one we've ever had!"

When Mary's family awoke that Christmas morning, they did so to the sound of bacon sizzling on the stove and the smell of hot cinnamon muffins coming from the little oven. There were bottles of syrup and jars of jam, and canned fruit, including kinds that the younger children had never even seen before. Every sock that was hanging was stuffed with homemade taffy, fudge, divinity, and dried fruit of every kind. The children didn't even know the names of some of the cookies and goodies that lay before them. Later Mary and Leland were to find tucked in each toe of the stockings that had been sent for them, a few dollars and a note stating that the money was to be used to buy coal and fuel for the rest of the winter, and oats and wheat to feed the animals.

For each boy there was a bag of marbles, and each girl had a little rag doll made just for her. But the most wonderful moment of the whole day was when Ellen awoke, the last to get up, and walked over to the spot where she had refused to hang her sock the night before. She rubbed her eyes in disbelief as she saw hanging there a beautiful red Christmas dress, trimmed with white and green satin ribbons. Ellen turned around, walked back to her bed, and lay down, thinking she was dreaming. After her little sisters pounced on her with laughter and excitement, she came back again to the celebration and joy of the most wonderful Christmas ever. For that morning, along with the aroma of good food, the love of a good family, and a new red dress, a childhood had been given back to a young girl—a child-hood of hopes and dreams, of Santa Claus, and of the wonder of Christmas.

I will never forget the retelling of this story by my mother, Mary Thomas Jeppson. Although it was always an emotional drain for her, it was an inspiration to all those who were privileged to hear her story every Christmas since that magical day in 1927.

—MARIAN JEPPSON WALKER
South Jordan, Utah

Merry Christmas,
Mrs. Moring

ANNY MORING HAD settled down to watch the eleven o'clock news in the den of his quiet home in Charleston, South Carolina. His children were tucked in bed. His wife, Allyson, who had complained of a bad case of the flu, was asleep at the other end of the house. Her illness was so severe—fever, chills, cramps, vomiting—that she had isolated herself so she would not pass along the bug to the rest of the family.

Suddenly Danny heard an odd scuffling noise in the kitchen. He went to look. There lay Allyson, curled on the floor in a fetal position. She had pulled herself all the way from their bedroom and now reached toward him, her face distorted in pain. "Danny, help me. I'm dying," she gasped, her teeth chattering. "I really am."

Her husband was stunned. Allyson, thirty-six, had enjoyed wonderful health—except recent surgery for a ruptured spinal disk. Only the day before, she, Danny, and their children—Elizabeth, nine, and Robert, one—had returned home from a Thanksgiving weekend camping trip.

Danny looked down at Allyson; the skin on her fingers and toes was turning purple. He carried her back to their bedroom and called 911. Then he stroked the wet, dark hair plastered to her face and hugged her icy body to him. Minutes later, when the emergency crew arrived, Allyson's blood pressure was undetectable. She was placed on a gurney and carried from the house. Standing in the doorway as the ambulance sped off into the night, Danny felt weak. Of all people, how could this be happening to Allyson? Danny phoned his father to come stay with the children, who were sound asleep. In his mind he could see them, snuggled in bed, innocent to the fact that the very heart of their lives had been plucked out and taken away.

For years now, with her high spirits and smiling slate-blue eyes, Mrs. Moring had won over the hearts of the fifty choral students at Bishop England High School where she taught. They loved to watch her drive into the parking lot, her head bobbing energetically as she filled the car with her own rendition of "I Could Have Danced All Night." Even at her most intense moments of conducting, her face was lit by a half smile.

Since her earliest days, Allyson had loved music. From the age of five, she had taken piano lessons, and later voice lessons. As a teacher, she believed that music could change lives for the better—that it could foster emotional development and enhance all the good aspects of life, the serious as well as the frivolous. She believed, too, that it could soothe those parts of life that are most difficult. In every sense, Allyson Moring was an apostle for the power of music.

For the 1994 Christmas concert, Mrs. Moring's group was attempting one of music's most difficult choral pieces, the "Hallelujah" chorus from Handel's *Messiah*. A challenge even for adults, the selection would be the centerpiece of the concert—if the students could get it right. For sixteen long weeks, the boys and girls had practiced after school, perfecting simpler selections and struggling with Handel's masterpiece. During Mrs. Moring's absence for back surgery, Katherine Allen, seventeen, a senior who had taken a course in directing music, filled in. But Katherine, slight of build with long blond hair, had found it hard to manage the large group. Believing she had failed as a conductor, she vowed she would stick to singing and leave directing to others.

Allyson Moring returned to choir practice, the success of her surgery marred only by a staph infection, for which she was given antibiotics. She finished the medication on Thanksgiving Saturday. Within hours, she had taken to bed with what she believed to be flu.

When Danny Moring reached the hospital, the news was brutally bad. Medicine's oldest enemy, massive systemic infection, also known as sepsis, had laid siege to his wife's body. She had gone into septic shock, in which bacteria overwhelm the body's systems, blood vessels begin to leak, and vital organs start shutting down. A doctor took Danny aside and suggested he gather the family. There was little chance that Allyson would survive the night.

The next afternoon, the choral group met to talk about

Mrs. Moring. The latest medical reports were dire. She had survived the night, but had been given the last rites by the parish priest. It would be almost impossible to stage the Christmas concert, only ten days away. But, more important, what could they do now for Mrs. Moring? One of the students had an idea.

Allyson Moring's infection raged on. At first, in her delirium, she had mumbled about the Christmas concert, telling Danny it had to go on. Then she became totally unresponsive, and was kept alive only by a respirator. Her body swelled so horribly with toxic fluids that her eyes disappeared into bloated flesh.

Danny was standing vigil at her bedside when two of Allyson's colleagues from Bishop England came to the intensive care unit and handed Danny an audiocassette. "From Allyson's students," they said.

Danny inserted the tape into a small player and turned it on. In a sudden burst, the joyful voices of girls and boys singing Christmas carols filled the cubicle. Staring into Allyson's face, Danny prayed that she could hear these voices that he knew she loved. Then his own heart jumped as he picked up the high, sweet refrain of one of her favorite songs: *"Do you hear what I hear? . . . Do you hear what I hear?"*

As Danny prayed for God to let Allyson hear, the singers suddenly began the "Hallelujah" chorus. What happened next astounded him. Allyson's eyelids twitched, and he felt a firm squeeze from her hand. Staring into Allyson's face, he thought he saw a tiny half-smile, as thrilling as any smile he had ever seen. Danny Moring wept with relief and knew that he would play the tape over and over. Then someone touched him on the shoulder. It was Allyson's father, pediatrician Dr. Allen Harrell. "Danny," he said gently, "I cannot let you get your hopes up. Allyson can't survive without a miracle." But there was no miracle. Pneumonia set in a few days later, and the illness grew worse.

"The tape made Mrs. Moring smile!" whooped one of the girls when Katherine came into the music room the next day. That spark of hope ignited the students. "There's no way we can *not* have the concert," said one of them. But who would conduct? All eyes were on Katherine Allen. "Never," said Katherine. "I'm not capable of it."

But efforts to find a substitute director failed. One night, Katherine and her mother talked until 1:00 A.M. Over and over, Katherine insisted, "I'm just not a conductor." But she couldn't stop thinking about Mrs. Moring. She remembered the powerful inspiration the teacher brought to their choral group—and the immense satisfaction they felt when she pushed them to their performing limits. The next morning, Katherine announced to her parents, "I've decided to do it."

On December 8, Charleston's magnificent Grace Episcopal Church opened its doors for the Bishop England Christmas concert. Word had spread about the students who were determined to fulfill their teacher's dream. More than five hundred people packed the seats and spilled into the foyer.

In another part of the church, Katherine and the chorus went over the difficult parts one last time. Finally, Katherine called for silence. "We are going to pray together for Mrs. Moring," she said. "And then we're going to go out there and make her proud." As she led the group in the Lord's Prayer, Katherine heard sobs. She struggled for composure herself.

In the darkened sanctuary of the Gothic church, the chorus, holding candles and singing "O Holy Night," made its way down the aisles. When the singers reached the front, the lights came up. Katherine could see Mrs. Moring's family in the front rows, their faces shining with the same hope the singers felt.

Steadying herself, she looked out over the crowd and informed them that their director was deathly ill. "We dedicate this concert to Mrs. Moring in the hope that she will get well," she said. Then Katherine turned and, with great flair, began the performance. As the voices intoned the familiar Christmas hymns, her confidence rose. But one thought continued to nag her: Could she keep them together for the finale? When the powerful opening to the "Hallelujah" chorus burst from the organ, Katherine took a deep breath and raised her arms. There was an excruciating pause. Then she flung her arms wide—and heard the voices explode, every note in place, warm and confident. Mrs. Moring's students were summoning sounds so pure that Handel's long crescendo of "hallelujahs" seemed to soar to the rafters, touching ears and hearts with the sound of heaven itself.

When silence finally fell, the listeners rose and broke into applause, some weeping and others crowding forward to embrace the singers. Exhausted, Katherine felt a hug at her waist. It was the Morings' little daughter, Elizabeth, embracing her as tightly as she could. Looking into the child's slate-blue eyes, Katherine was overcome with joy.

That same night, less than a mile from the church, Danny Moring sat holding his wife's hand, the tape made by her students still playing. Allyson's condition remained hopeless. Danny didn't even know whether the news of the successful Christmas concert had penetrated her unconsciousness. But slowly, remarkably, over the next few days, her systems began to stabilize. Lungs and kidneys started functioning. Allyson began to recover.

On Christmas morning, just seventeen days after the concert, Allyson sat quietly in her own living room. Baby Robert squirmed in her lap as Danny and Elizabeth fetched presents from beneath the tree. Allyson was bone thin and exhausted, but her face wore a radiant smile. Why she got well, or even when the precise turning point came, is not important to Allyson Moring. The key fact is that her long, tortured slumber was filled with music. "What I remember is music, music, music—the beautiful music and voices that I loved."

Soon after Mrs. Moring got home, Katherine Allen and several others from the choral group tapped gingerly on her door, bearing gifts and flowers. There was an explosion of emotion as the girls and Mrs. Moring hugged one another. She told the girls what she had told so many—that the entire experience has certified her faith in God's power through music and prayer and the wonderful capacity of young people.

Today Allyson Moring, completely recovered, is busy putting final touches on this year's Bishop England Christmas concert. If the most precious of God's gifts is life, the Morings have realized a blessing every bit as special to them as

Allyson's recovery—a baby boy born to them in October. Merry Christmas, Mrs. Moring.

—ALLYSON MORING
Charleston, South Carolina
As told to Henry Hurt

Icy Water Rescue

I T WAS SATURDAY, December 28, 1996. My best friend, Candi Peterson, and I were on Christmas vacation from the fifth grade, and had been having a wonderful time. The winter weather had been un-usually harsh, and the night before it had snowed about two feet in our little town of La Conner, Washington, on the Puget Sound. Snow is rare where we live: It only comes once every few years. I'd spent the night at Candi's, and we viewed the situation with delight. The snow seemed like a last-minute Christmas present from God!

As soon as we were up that morning, we climbed into our heavy snowsuits and headed outside with a sled. First we went sledding down the hill by Candi's house. Then we headed over to sled on the small hills of the golf course, next to the marina. The water at the marina was covered in a thin layer of ice and looked really cool—we just had to get a closer look. The docks were off limits to us—we knew we should have an adult and life jackets to go down to the docks and be around the boats, but all we planned to do was look at the icy water. It seemed safe enough.

As we started down the ramp, I got a little scared because the docks were covered with snow. It was hard to see where the sides of the ramp ended, but I kept on going. We sat down on the narrow, snow-covered dock and put the sled out on the ice to see if it would break—it didn't. We moved to another part of the dock to test it again—we wanted to see the ice break! The ice wouldn't break there either, so we ended our science experiment and decided to go back and sled at the golf course as we'd originally planned. I got up and turned around to leave. But as Candi got up to leave, her feet slipped off the dock, pitching her into the icy water.

I heard the splash, turned around, and screamed, "Candi!" She was in the cold, slushy water a few feet off the dock, trying hard to keep her head above water. I ran back to her, not thinking about anything except that she would die if I couldn't get her out. I lay down on my stomach and managed to grab her hands but I didn't have the strength to pull her out. She was so heavy, weighed down by a snowsuit and heavy boots. We both screamed for help, but no one was around to hear us. I tried again to pull her out but just couldn't get her out of the water. I asked her if she could hold on while I ran for help. "No," she said. "Please don't leave me, Holly."

Her boots had come off under the water by now, and her teeth were chattering. She was very cold.

I stood up and looked around the docks behind me one more time, hoping to see an adult with the strength to pull her out. There was no one. Realizing that I was Candi's only hope, I lay down on the dock to try again to pull her out.

My two earlier attempts to pull Candi out had left me exhausted and my arms aching. I knew that I had only one more try before she drowned. So I closed my eyes for a fraction of a second and prayed. I prayed that I would have the strength to pull my best friend out of the water. And suddenly, I could feel the presence of someone else there with me, someone who would give me the strength and courage to save my friend's life.

In an effort to keep from falling in myself, I hooked my foot under a rope cleat on the dock to give myself a solid anchor. Candi was farther away from the dock now. I could no longer reach her hands, but by stretching out as far as I could, I managed to grab the end of her wool scarf floating on the surface. I said another prayer and I pulled, and despite the fact that the first two tries had left me feeling weak, this time I seemed to get stronger and stronger as I worked. Slowly I pulled her out of the water and onto the dock. I unzipped her snowsuit and pulled her wet clothes off. Growing up around the water, I knew all about hypothermia and how quickly it could happen. Candi and I were both sobbing with relief now, but she was still freezing cold and frightened. I put her on the sled and pulled her up the ramp as quickly as I could to find a public phone. We found one; I called the operator and, still crying, told her our troubles. She put me through to Candi's mother Cheri. Due to the snow and ice, Cheri couldn't bring her car down the hill and had to run down the hill in order to find us. As we waited for her help, I tried to keep Candi as warm as I could by wrapping her in my coat and hugging her. When Candi's mom arrived, we both pulled Candi up the hill on her sled to her house. Cheri immediately put Candi into a hot bath to warm her up.

Candi did not suffer any ill effects from her ordeal. Later, when she and I talked about what had happened, she said that she had felt sure that she was going to die there in the icy water. I told her about my prayers, and that I knew that there was someone watching over us out there that day. Instead of getting weaker from pulling, I had gotten stronger. A big topic at United Methodist, the church my family attends in La Conner, is guardian angels. I just know that there was a guardian angel out there on the dock that day, helping me save Candi.

—HOLLY DEGROOT
La Conner, Washington

Note: Holly, age twelve, was later given a certificate for bravery by the Swinomish Police Department for her icy water rescue.

The Gold and
Ivory Tablecloth

AT CHRISTMASTIME MEN and women every-where gather in their churches to wonder anew at the greatest miracle the world has ever known. But the story I like to recall was not a miracle—not exactly.

It happened to a pastor who was very young. His church was very old. Once, long ago, it had flourished. Famous men had preached from its pulpit, prayed before its altar. Rich and poor alike had worshiped there and built it hopefully. Now the good days had passed from the section of town where it stood. But the young pastor and his wife believed in their run-down church. They felt that with paint, hammer, and faith they could get it into shape. Together they went to work.

But late in December a severe storm whipped through the area and the worst blow fell on the little church. A huge chunk of rain-soaked plaster fell out of the inside wall just behind the altar. Sorrowfully the pastor and his wife swept away the mess, but they couldn't hide the ragged hole.

The pastor looked at it and had to remind himself quickly, "Thy will be done!" But his wife wept, "Christmas is only two days away!"

That afternoon the dispirited couple attended an auction held for the benefit of a youth group. The auctioneer opened a box and shook out of its folds a handsome gold and ivory lace tablecloth. It was a magnificent item, nearly fifteen feet long. But it, too, dated from a long-vanished era. Who, to-day, had any use for such a thing? There were a few half-hearted bids. Then the pastor was seized with what he thought was a great idea. He bought it for $6.50.

He carried the cloth back to the church and tacked it up on the wall behind the altar. It completely hid the hole! And the extraordinary beauty of its shimmering handwork cast a fine holiday glow over the chancel. It was a great triumph. Happily he went back to preparing his Christmas sermon.

Just before noon on Christmas Eve, as the pastor was opening the church, he noticed a woman standing in the cold at the bus stop.

"The bus won't be here for forty minutes," he called, and he invited her into the church to get warm.

She told him that she had come from the city that morning to be interviewed for a job as governess to the children of one of the wealthy families in town but she had been turned down. A war refugee, her English was imperfect.

The woman sat down in the pew and chafed her hands and rested. After a while she dropped her head and prayed.

She looked up as the pastor began to adjust the great gold and ivory lace cloth across the hole. She rose suddenly and walked up the steps of the chancel. She looked at the tablecloth. The pastor smiled and started to tell her about the storm damage, but she didn't seem to listen. She took up a fold of the cloth and rubbed it between her fingers.

"It is mine!" she said. "It is my banquet cloth!" She lifted up a corner and showed the surprised pastor that there were initials monogrammed on it. "My husband had the cloth made especially for me in Brussels! There could not be another like it!"

For the next few minutes the woman and the pastor talked excitedly together. She explained that she was Viennese; that she and her husband had opposed the Nazis and decided to leave the country. They were advised to go separately. Her husband put her on a train for Switzerland. They planned that he would join her as soon as he could arrange to ship their household goods across the border.

She never saw him again. Later she heard that he had died in a concentration camp.

"I have always felt that it was my fault—to leave without him," she said. "Perhaps these years of wandering have been my punishment."

The pastor tried to comfort her, urged her to take the cloth. She refused. Then she went away.

As the church began to fill on Christmas Eve, it was clear that the cloth was going to be a great success. It had been skillfully designed to look its best by candlelight.

After the service, the pastor stood in the doorway; many people told him that the church looked beautiful. One gentle-faced, middle-aged man—he was the local watch and clock repairman—looked rather puzzled.

"It is strange," he said in his soft accent. "Many years ago my wife—God rest her—and I owned such a cloth. In our home in Vienna, my wife put it on the table"—and here he smiled—"only when the bishop came to dinner."

The pastor became very excited. He told the jeweler about the woman who had been in the church earlier in the day.

The startled jeweler clutched the pastor's arm. "Can it be? Does she live?"

Together the two got in touch with the family who had interviewed her. Then, in the pastor's car, they started for the city. And as Christmas Day was born, this man and his wife—who had been separated through the many saddened Yuletides—were reunited.

To all who heard this story, the joyful purpose of the storm that had knocked a hole in the wall of the church was now quite clear. Of course, people said it was a miracle, but I think you will agree it was the season for it!

—REV. HOWARD C. SCHADE
Nyack, New York

"The Gold and Ivory Tablecloth." Reprinted with permission from the December 1954 *Reader's Digest*. Copyright © by The Reader's Digest Assn., Inc.

Second Chance

CHRISTMAS HAS ALWAYS been a very special time of year for the McKinnon household. We didn't always have a lot of gifts, but the holiday had deeper meaning for us than just opening presents. Christmas was about family get-togethers with music, laughter, and feasting on our mother's wonderful cooking after our father's prayer of thanksgiving.

December 1977 looked to be no different. Preparations were well under way for another great family get-together, and everyone wondered excitedly who would draw whose name in our gift selection game. On December 15, my sixty-five-year-old mother Lula told me her doctor wanted her to check into the hospital to investigate her irregular heartbeat. Nothing serious, she assured me. It was just routine.

As I drove her to the hospital, my mother remembered something about the previous August when my wife, Patrice, and I came to my mother and father to tell them the news that we were expecting our first child. I'm not sure why, but as Mother spoke, a dark thought occurred to me: My own grandmother Ellen had died shortly before *my* birth. Would the same fate await our unborn child's grandmother?

The day after Mother checked in, I was shocked to get a call that I should go to the hospital as soon as possible. The young woman from patient services was compassionate as she led me to Mother's physician. I had faced many crisis situations during my military and law enforcement careers. But there is little one can do to prepare for the moment a doctor tells you that your mother has suffered two heart attacks and a stroke.

I thought it might be a bad dream. She'd only been at the hospital overnight for some tests. How could this happen in the hospital? My sister Gloria arrived and I listened again as the doctor explained that our mother wasn't responding. He suggested that we speak to her; perhaps the sound of her children's voices could bring her out of it.

Entering the critical care unit we saw tubes protruding from Mother's nose and mouth, and machines bleeping away, monitoring her feeble life signs. Gloria turned away. "I can't see her this way," she said. I approached the bed, grabbed my mother's hand, and called her name repeatedly. I got no response. I tried again and again. My frustration showed, and the doctor pulled us away to deliver more grim news.

"In her condition and at her age, there is a strong possibility that she may not recover," he said as kindly as he could. His calm professionalism put me at ease and helped me steel myself for telling the rest of the family. I asked the doctor if there was anything I could do to help. "Pray for a Christmas miracle," he said.

I drifted down the corridor, trying to gather my thoughts. I stumbled into the hospital chapel, slid into a short pew, and began to pray. For the next several days, I would arrive at my mother's bedside, grasp her hand, and talk to her. I told her how Patrice's pregnancy was going and what I thought about my job with the police department. After an hour or more, I'd retreat to the chapel where the family gathered: my sisters Gloria, Ada, Helen, Bernice, and, of course, our father, Cota McKinnon.

My father's prayers were always out loud. Father, the head deacon at Weeping Willow Baptist Church, would ask for his wife's recovery and always end by saying, "I pray for Jesus' sake."

Two days before Christmas, I got a call from Gloria. She was exuberant. "Guess what? Ma is up and talking," she said, almost hyperventilating. I dropped the phone and hurried over. Ma was propped up in the hospital bed and seemed to be having a wonderful time talking to everyone.

She spoke of losing weight. She couldn't wait to get home and fix her own meals because she didn't like hospital food. She knew she wouldn't be home in time for our Christmas Day celebration, but she gave explicit instructions to my sisters about how to fix Father's favorite Christmas meal. When I saw my mother's doctor, he said, "Maybe this is your miracle."

It was an incredible day. All of us had given up hope that we'd ever speak with our mother again, yet there she was, being her usual animated self. We all went home feeling blessed. Early the next morning, Christmas Eve, yet another phone call came from the hospital. "Get back here immediately," they said.

When I got there, the doctor's head was low. "You've got bad news," I said.

"Yes," the doctor said. "Your mother just passed." As the rest of the family began arriving and tears began to flow, I thought about how I'd hoped for a Christmas miracle that would save Mother. And in the sadness that engulfed our family that day, it slowly occurred to me that indeed we had had our miracle. Our mother had been gone, but she had come back to us for one full joyous day. Our entire family had had a second chance to share our love with our mother. That was our miracle.

—ISAIAH MCKINNON
Chief, Detroit Police Department

The Kiss

I N *MY FAIR LADY*, the arrogant but charming
Henry Higgins attempts to teach Eliza an important lesson when he says, "The greatest secret, Eliza . . .
is in having the same manners for all human souls; in short,
behaving as though you were in heaven, where there are no
third-class carriages, and one soul is as good as another." For
most of us, it is easy to love those we admire and those who
return our affection, but the big test in life comes in caring
for those who are somewhat difficult to love and who give
nothing in return—the stranger, the less powerful, the poor,
the unimportant. I learned that lesson one Christmas many
years ago when we lived in California.

I was in charge of a woman's organization in my church
for several years. Part of my responsibility was to look after
the sick and elderly, giving compassionate service to those
in need.

I was told there was a woman in our area who was unable

to attend church because of health problems and who needed some assistance. Two other women from the church joined me to visit her to see how we could help her. Margaret was a small Danish woman with a slight accent, almost blind from diabetes and very arthritic. She lived alone and had two grown children who hardly ever came to see her. From the minute we met her, we could sense that she was a very proud and independent woman, and that she was uncomfortable and embarrassed to ask for our help. She had owned her own business for many years—a very fine dress shop—and a few of the beautiful wedding gowns she sold still hung in plastic bags in her closets. Despite her rather cold and formal demeanor, we could see that she badly needed our assistance.

We spent many days there over the next year. We would come in the morning and straighten her apartment; then we would fix lunch and try to leave something for her dinner. She would thank us very properly, never showing any real emotion; we sensed she had grown lonely and bitter over the years and had learned to keep herself at a distance from the rest of the world. We tried very hard to be caring and loving, but we always left wondering if she even appreciated anything we had done. All in all, it was not a very gratifying experience; Margaret simply would not let us love her.

Time went on, Margaret's health deteriorated, and finally she was put into a nursing home. I hadn't seen her for some months and was feeling a little guilty about it. It was December and I was caught up in the mad dash of the holiday season: parties, shopping, Christmas cards, decorating, and many other activities to squeeze in before the big day. My sisters and I had been invited to a Christmas luncheon, an annual event I looked forward to each year. It was a very elegant affair in Beverly Hills and it was fun to get dressed up and mingle with some of the well-known people who attended. On this particular December day, however, I had a nagging feeling that I needed to cancel my luncheon plans and instead pay a visit to Margaret. As I dutifully walked from my parked car to her drab-looking nursing home, I kept wondering what had compelled me to give up my favorite party to visit a woman I didn't really know or even particularly like. I was full of resentment and was feeling a bit like a martyr. I certainly wasn't doing this act of kindness for the right reasons.

My own mother had lived the last five years of her life in a nursing home, stricken with such severe arthritis that she remained in a fetal position most of the time. I had spent many hours there visiting her; now the all-too-familiar smells and sounds of another nursing home brought back bittersweet memories. As I stood by Margaret's bedside and looked down at her face, she reminded me very much of my own mother, who was half Danish—the same fair complexion and very blue eyes. As I reflected on my mother for a moment, I remembered what I used to do when I visited her. I asked Margaret if I could put lotion on her hands.

"Oh, please do," she quietly answered. I began to massage her thin, gnarled hands that looked so much like my mother's. Then I put a little lotion on her face and neck and rubbed some on her back. I picked up a brush and brushed her white hair and tried to make it look pretty. She began to relax and seemed to enjoy the attention and intimacy, something I thought this proud and unfriendly woman could never do.

Suddenly as I was rubbing more lotion on her arms, she grabbed my hand and looked up at me with her weary old eyes. "Kiss me," she whispered. "Kiss me." A little surprised, I smiled, leaned down, and kissed her softly. Then she said, "Oh, again, please." I kissed her on the other cheek and I noticed tears in her eyes. It was as if my simple kisses were melting away the layers of cold, hard exterior that had built up over all her years of loneliness. I suddenly found myself kissing her again and again all over her face as we cried together. I gave her a warm embrace that she desperately clung to and I assured her I'd come back again soon. As I turned to go, the realization dawned on me: Here was an old woman whose children had all but abandoned her, but whose hunger for the human touch was so intense that she would reach out to a mere acquaintance for any loving gesture that could feed her starving soul. At that moment, I felt honored to be the one to meet that need.

I walked out of the hospital on cloud nine, feeling like I had been transformed. The pure joy of the true Christmas spirit filled my heart and soul as it never had before. I now realized why I had decided to forgo my luncheon that day: There were more important people to be with and lives to touch than would ever be possible in an elegant restaurant filled with celebrities. I wasn't sure why I had felt such an urgency about the matter—perhaps the urgency was for me.

I remember a story I once heard, in which one of the innkeepers who couldn't find room for Joseph and Mary on that first Christmas night, later said in his own defense,

"What could be done? The inn was full of folk—and there were just two of them—no servants, just a workman sort of man leading a donkey and his wife thereon, drooping and pale. I saw them not myself, my servants having driven them away; but if I had seen them, how was I to know? Should innkeepers welcome stragglers in all our towns from Beer-sheba to Dan, in case He should come? There was a sign, they say, a heavenly light resplendent, but I had no time for stars; and there were songs of angels in the air out on the hills. But how was I to hear amid the thousand clamors of an inn?"

Fortunately for me that day, I had put the clamors of the world aside, and for a few brief moments had witnessed the star's heavenly light and felt the angels' song. The memory of that kiss planted on a weary old woman's sweet face, cultivated by human tears, has grown and enlarged each new Christmas with a love for all mankind that I never knew possible. I had learned for myself that the gift of a loving heart at Christmas is truly the greatest gift of all.

—OLIVIA PRATT
Bronxville, New York

The Gift

HIS PAST CHRISTMAS I received an extraordinary gift, a miraculous and selfless gift from someone I barely knew. For many years I have had lupus, and last year my doctors told me that as a result of the lupus my kidneys were failing. I was facing a future in which thrice-weekly dialysis would become a fact of life, unless I underwent a kidney transplant. My family and friends rallied around me and took medical tests in order to determine whether any of them could donate a healthy kidney. After many weeks of forms and tests, we received the crushing news that, because of my O-positive blood type, no one I knew was a potential kidney donor for me. "We will add you right away to the list of kidney patients in the country awaiting transplants," my medical team told me. "But the wait could be as long as three years. Your kidneys will fail long before that." I was devastated by that news, and even more disheartened to hear on the car radio that same day of the sudden death of humorist Erma Bombeck during a kidney transplant operation.

Despite this grim news I still needed to take care of the small chores that are a part of everyday living, and so it was that I went into the bank to make a deposit, still reeling from the information I'd received. "Miki, are you all right?" my favorite bank teller asked me. My sad tale rushed out of me there in the bank lobby. I unloaded detail after detail to a woman I barely knew. We'd chatted casually over the three years I'd banked at that branch, mainly about art. I am a painter and the bank teller is a dancer, so we'd connected as artists in some small way, but she knew nothing of my medical struggles.

"And no one in my family is a match! I could wait three years before a kidney is found for me!" She sympathized over my plight and asked a few polite questions about the transplant process before I finished up my banking business and went on to the next errand.

Several weeks later I met again with my doctors to discuss the situation. "So," they said, smiling broadly, "tell us about your donor!"

"Donor? I don't have a donor, you know that. No one was a match for me."

The head doctor looked confused, and looked down at some papers he held. "Yes, we have it right here. Mary Groves is her name."

"I don't know anyone named Mary Groves," I protested.

"Yes," the doctors insisted, "Mary Groves. It says here that she is your bank teller and a dancer."

And then it hit me. "Oh my God!" I burst out crying, suddenly remembering that day in the bank when I'd told her about my situation. What on earth had inspired her to decide that she, a woman who barely knew me, would willingly undergo major surgery and donate one of her healthy kidneys to me?

Mary told me that she felt she'd been chosen to help me. "God is providing for you through me," she said. "I'm receiving this as a gift, too—I'm getting to do this for you. This is a God-given thing, when He asks you to do something He gives you the tools to do it—the people and the peace of mind."

After many more months of testing (it was a match!) and soul-searching, the transplant took place in San Francisco on December 10, 1996. We both sailed through, even though as the donor the surgery was more invasive for Mary than it was for me. We met incredible people there in the transplant unit of the hospital. The walls were hung with photographs of folks smiling and hugging each other—loving pairs of people just like us who had gone through this procedure together.

Mary and I have a special bond, after all we've been through together. My dream is that we will someday be able to mount an exhibition together; I will do the abstract paintings and Mary will dance. I want to get her name out into the world—Mary Groves—to let everyone know how special she is and what she has done. Her generosity and my life-and-death experience have changed my whole outlook on life. No matter how horrible the news is on television, I know that there are special people in the world like Mary Groves, people who are guardian angels for the rest of us.

—MIKI HSU LEAVEY
Napa, California

Ten-Candy-Bar Christmas

I T WAS 1987, and my girls and I were going to have our first Christmas together since we'd become a single-parent family. And we were broke.

The fact that we could pay our monthly bills was cause for celebration—but there would be no extras that year. I explained to my daughters that we could afford a bare Christmas tree, but that, for the first time in their young lives, there would be no gifts underneath it. "This is going to be a Top Ramen and Kool-Aid Christmas, girls," I explained. We were poor but we were happy, and the three of us set about making ornaments out of paper scraps and aluminum foil to brighten up the way our bare apartment looked.

I'd been taking the bus to work (the old family car could go only so far), and a few days before Christmas my girls came down to the bus stop to meet me, faces shining with excitement. "There's a turkey raffle, Mom! We heard about it on the radio and we called up and entered! I bet we win the turkey—you just wait and see!" Such sweet little optimists they were, not yet worn out by life's bad luck as I was. I smiled and patted them on their shoulders and agreed that, yes, it would be wonderful if we won the turkey mentioned on the radio.

I went to work as usual on Christmas Eve. Mine was not what you would call a challenging job, but it kept a roof over our heads during those tough times. Not much happened at work on the day before Christmas. Most of the other employees had taken the day off to do a little last-minute shopping and the office was very quiet. Midway through the day the phone rang. "Cathe, it's for you," the receptionist said. "Somebody from a radio station." We'd won the turkey after all! The girls and I hauled that big, cold bird home on the bus, singing Christmas carols and giggling the whole way back to the apartment.

The apartment complex that we lived in that year was filled with other mothers in the same financial situation as I, with not much other than the love we had for our kids to keep us warm at night. So we decided to invite some of the other single moms and their kids to join us for our feast of—you guessed it—roast turkey, Top Ramen, and Kool-Aid. It was a wonderful meal we all shared together.

After the dishes had been cleared and the girls had gone off to visit friends in another apartment, I heard a light tap on our door. I opened it. No one was there. An envelope fell to the ground; it had been stuck in the door frame. No note, no greeting, but inside the envelope were two worn dollar bills. I suspected that this was the only way one of the other moms knew to thank us for sharing the Christmas turkey. I looked up and down the hallway for a hint of our benefactor, but all of the doors were closed tight. Suddenly, I had a wild idea.

With the girls occupied for the next hour or two, I slipped on my coat and headed out to the local discount store—the "ninety-eight-cent store." I raced down in the hope that it was still open this late at night—and yes! It was! I could hardly contain my zeal as I cruised the aisles, trying to decide how to stretch my two dollars into the best Christmas gifts I could. And then I saw the candy aisle. I never let the girls have candy, so this would be a crazy surprise. With my two dollars I was able to buy twenty candy bars—ten for each of my daughters.

I ran home, hoping they were still out. Searching the apartment for gift wrap I came up empty-handed, but I did find plenty of typing paper. I pulled out the kids' crayons and decorated the paper to my heart's content, carefully drawing gold and silver stars and Christmas trees to make it look as festive as possible. And then I wrapped each one of those twenty candy bars into a miniature Christmas gift and spread them all out underneath the homely little tree. It looked like Santa had come after all.

When the girls came home, they shouted with delight to see gifts under the tree. "Don't get too excited now, it's all I could afford. . . ." But the girls carried on with such joy at every candy bar they unwrapped that you would have thought they were opening the best toys F.A.O. Schwarz had to offer. We hugged and laughed and sat down at the table together to share the candy bars and continue our holiday feast.

We awakened Christmas morning with loving hearts and the miracle of each other, together and happy despite all we'd been through with the divorce that year. My girls and I have never forgotten our "ten-candy-bar Christmas" and the magical appearance of, first, a turkey, and then, two dollars, which made it such a special time.

—CATHE ODOM
Sacramento, California

Homeless Santa

CRUMMY 1988 was winding down as my roommate Margaret Cable and I set out for an afternoon snack on Christmas Eve. I'd just returned to California after a dark three months of hiding in the Swedish woods in my own private Ingmar Bergman film after the breakup of a long-term romance. My arrival home had been as dramatic as my sudden departure some months before. I was booked on a Pan Am flight from London to San Francisco. Having been away from home for three months, I was so anxious to get home for Christmas that I told myself if I missed the flight I would take the next available flight, Pan Am 103. I made my flight with just minutes to spare. Passengers for the San Francisco flight were checking in at a counter directly across from the New York flight, but I absentmindedly got into the wrong line with the New York–bound folks. When I noticed my mistake, I joked about it to the people in line and made my way across the room.

As my parents drove home from the airport over slow-moving California freeways, they told me about the midair explosion of Flight 103 over Lockerbee, Scotland. "But I saw those people," I said. "How can they all be dead?" My dreams that night were haunted by the image of the Scottish countryside strewn with carefully packed Christmas gifts, steamed puddings from Harrod's, and little piles of Christmas candy that an airport Santa had handed to everyone waiting in line to go through the security X ray.

After such a close brush with death I was feeling a little peculiar on that bright California afternoon, a little tentative and oddly disconnected to what was going on around me. I'd come home after an absence of three months, but I didn't feel like I'd come back in one piece.

Craving the taste of authentic Mexican food, Margaret and I chose to head for a ramshackle burrito house in a dicey part of town. Near the train tracks and several homeless shelters, it was not a part of town you'd expect to find two middle-class girls visiting on Christmas Eve. We ordered our burritos and sat outside in the sun. The streets around us were deserted; office workers and commuters had gone home to get an early start on the holiday.

Margaret nudged my arm. "Oh great," she said. "Looks like we're about to get hit up for money." A disheveled man was making his way toward us through the parking lot of the burrito house, his progress slowed both by his age and by the oversized green sack he carried on his back. His hair was long and snowy white, his thick beard spread over the top of his tattered jacket. Margaret and I clucked our tongues and shook our heads and began to search our pockets for loose change in order to dispense with him quickly and get on with our meal.

Slowly and quietly he made his way across the blacktop until he was standing in front of us. He stopped, and without saying a word he rolled his heavy bag off his shoulder and set it on the ground before us. Untying the top, he reached in and began to rummage through the contents of his bag. Margaret and I watched as he found what he was seeking and removed his hand. He held a shiny red apple. In total silence and with great dignity he held the apple out to Margaret. She reached out and accepted his gift. He reached into his green duffel bag again and this time pulled out a Snickers bar and offered it to me. "No," I said. "We can't take your food; you need it." Margaret and I both held our new gifts back out to him. "We can't take your food." The man smiled shyly and shook his head. "I can't eat it. My teeth are no good. Merry Christmas."

He would not accept the money we tried to give him that afternoon; he just kept quietly shaking his head and smiling as we tried to press dollar bills into his hand. Finally, he agreed to the purchase of a cup of coffee for him. He took the steaming Styrofoam container and, shouldering his bag once again, continued on his way.

I think about that homeless man whenever I pass down that street. I think about the quiet man with the big white beard and the bag of presents who gave two privileged girls part of the only food he had. The spirit of giving is all around us and can come upon us so unexpectedly. We need to be able to give back what we can to those who need it most.

—JENNIFER BASYE SANDER
Granite Bay, California

The Secret Dolls

I HAD BEEN a single mother for years, raising five sons. Now I was remarried to David, a widower, and I was feeling a little awkward in David's family home. Making the adjustment was a challenge for both me and my new family, which included David's three grown-up daughters.

As December approached, I felt apprehensive when I thought of the holidays. None of my own children would make it home for Christmas, and I wanted David's children to know that I loved them and was happy to be a part of their family. What could I give them?

When we had first gotten married in September, I had begun investigating and reorganizing the house so I would know where things were and so I would feel more at home. One day, I found an old shoebox covered with dust. Inside, packed in shredded newspapers, were parts for three porcelain dolls. I was startled and pleased. I knew that David's first wife, Lois, had loved working with ceramics. Her daughter-in-law once mentioned that Lois had even begun some ceramic dolls for her three daughters, but the figures had never been finished. Were these the dolls Lois had begun?

I thought of David's daughters and my longing to be their friend. Could I somehow finish the dolls and present them as a Christmas gift, not only from me but from their own loving mother? Ecstatic, I told David of my discovery, and he shared my excitement. First, I took the dolls to Linda, a doll expert whom a friend had recommended. She was astonished at the delicate pieces and agreed to finish them by painting and firing the ceramic parts, assembling the dolls, and making dresses. I chose dress colors that I thought matched each daughter's personality. Each doll would have a slightly different shade of auburn hair.

Upon my return home, the phone was ringing. It was Linda, her voice filled with emotion. "Do you know these dolls have been dedicated?" she asked me.

"What's a dedicated doll?"

"On each doll's ceramic body appears an inscription: 'To my dear Kathy,' 'To my dear Heidi,' 'To my dear Lorelee.' Each is signed, 'Love, Mom, 1970.' "

Like Lois's hand from the past, I thought. The dedications made the dolls even more precious, and I looked forward to giving them to David's daughters. I now realized that Lois had poured the ceramic parts for those dolls fourteen long years before, when the youngest girl, Lorelee, had been only five years old.

Finally the dolls were ready. I had written a note to each of the girls, telling them about my feelings for them and explaining why the dolls were so important. I emphasized that each doll came from two mothers who loved them a great deal—their own mom and me. I bought gift boxes, nested the dolls in tissue paper, added the notes, and wrapped everything carefully. I was more excited about those dolls than about any other gifts I was giving. So was David.

The next day, we assembled the children, their spouses, the grandchildren, and the cousins for our presentation. Wordlessly, David and I gave each daughter her package. They began unwrapping them. Silence, then gasps, sobs, and floods of tears. Somehow, even Lois seemed to be there.

Lorelee threw her arms around me. Later, Heidi confided that the doll confirmed to her that I was supposed to be part of their family circle. Kathy wrote a note expressing how touched she was and how meaningful the doll would always be to her. And through this gift of love from Lois and myself, I finally felt the acceptance and the comfort of being a real part of David's family.

—MarGene B. Lyon
Salt Lake City, Utah

My Shiny Fire Truck

IKE MOST CHILDREN, I asked for toys every Christmas. But the most memorable present for me was the bright red fire engine that came Christmas Eve 1970. Now this big, red hook and ladder was not in a box or decorated with a bow. It was, however, waiting for me when I got home.

Every Christmas Eve my whole family bundled up and went to midnight Mass. This particular year, my little sister was home with the chicken pox. She had such a high fever and outbreak of sores that my father decided to stay home with her.

As the rest of us put on our coats, my mother made sure that Dad and Tracy were as comfortable as possible. The lights were turned down or off; goodies on the table were covered; everything was ready for us to go.

I remember that the dining room table looked so beautiful, laden with all the food we were going to eat when we returned. On the mantel was a centerpiece that my mother had received as a gift: four tall red candles surrounded by holly and berries on a plastic base. All the cards and artwork that we children had made circled the candles for a complete holiday theme.

As we drove off, Dad was in his easy chair with a nice fire going, the lights of the Christmas tree filled the room with color, and my sister was asleep on the couch.

Christmas Eve is a wonderful time. Mass, as usual, was overwhelming with the choir, a full congregation, and the priests dressed in magnificent robes. We sang, shared, and prayed. I was hoping that my sister would feel better. I mean, what a time to be sick! Santa was coming; Christ was born; it was a holiday for family, friends, food, and, of course, presents.

My mother, brothers, and I had stopped by our friends' house for some holiday cheer before heading for home. We didn't stay long, knowing that Dad and Tracy were waiting for us. Besides, we always got to open one present before Santa brought us the real loot in the middle of the night. We said our good-byes and sang carols all the way home.

As we were busy singing and trying to remember the words, we braked at the light down the street from our house. In the distance we could see big trucks in the middle of the street. Suddenly, silence descended in our car. Only the pounding of hearts was heard. It was hard to believe what we saw, or what we thought we saw. I think my mother sat through two green lights. We all knew that we should make the sign of the cross if we ever heard or saw a siren because someone might need our prayers—but us? I mean, things like this happen to other people, and how could anything like this possibly happen on Christmas Eve?

As we drew nearer, we realized that those big trucks—those big, bright, red trucks—were in front of our house. The firemen were packing up their gear. On the porch two dark figures stood trembling. Only the whites of their eyes and teeth showed through the soot.

I could feel my knees get weak as I imagined what they were feeling. The tears streaming down their faces began to wash the bits and pieces of soot from their cheeks. Between those tears, my sister tried to tell us what had taken place during the last hour.

The same centerpiece that mother had so carefully placed on the mantel, up and out of reach of young hands, had been left with the candles burning. Within the time we were gone, the candles had burned down to the holly and berries, melting the plastic base with so much heat that all the cards and artwork had gone up in flames.

My sister awoke to find the room filled with smoke. She tried to call my father's name, but began choking on the fumes. She could hear him coughing nearby, but he was not responding to her cries. She crawled on the floor over to his chair and began shaking him, but he was not coming to. My sister dragged him to the front door and laid him on the cold porch outside. Nine years old and weak from fever, she had had the strength of two men.

One of the neighbors saw the commotion and called for help. Within seconds, the firemen responded to the call. The house was badly damaged by the smoke, but all the walls were still standing and two lives were saved.

The thought of losing another family member was unbearable to us. Several years earlier, we had lost an important member of our close-knit family, and the holidays ever since had always seemed to lack something or someone. As soon as reality hit that, yes, my father and sister were alive and well—dirty but happy to be alive—our natural senses of humor came through. Making jokes at the oddest moments has helped us get through so many rough times. Standing there on the lawn, mother laughed at being blamed for burning the pies again and for not dusting as well as usual. With my family gathered around each other and the firemen looking on, I thanked Santa for giving me the best and biggest fire engine a kid could ever ask for.

—KIT DILLON GIVAS
Carmichael, California

Circle of Love

AS WE GROW older, we come to realize that one of the genuine gifts of childhood is the magical way that a small child views even the simplest thing. The memory of opening our first pop-up book, finding the hidden toy in the Cracker Jack box, or riding a bike without training wheels—each of these events seems like magic at the time.

Much of the magic in my early years was provided by the gifts of two glamorous aunts, Aunt Lupe and Aunt Mary. My mother Vivian was one of twelve children of a pear farming family in the Sacramento River Delta. Her sisters lavished toys and attention on my sister and me; we were the sole beneficiaries of their undivided love and devotion.

Aunt Lupe was particularly exotic. She lived in Palm Springs, and to a seven-year-old like me, that seemed the very pinnacle of sophistication and elegance. Her frequent letters and postcards were exciting and colorful and told of fancy parties, perpetually sunny skies and swimsuit weather, and frequent sightings of famous movie stars. Like clockwork the gifts from Palm Springs would arrive for our birthdays and at Christmas. Her carefully selected gifts brought joy and contentment to our young lives. Someone from far away loved and cherished us, and it made us feel tremendously special.

In the mid-1960s Aunt Lupe truly outdid herself. Showing the sixth sense she seemed to have for our interests, that year she sent us each a beautiful satin-lined ivory jewelry box with hand-painted pink flowers and gold trim. When the box was opened, a delicate plastic ballerina spun around on one foot to the tune of the "Blue Danube Waltz."

But there was an even more wonderful surprise tucked inside the pink satin lining: a piece of costume jewelry, a Christmas pin that was the most perfect thing I had ever seen in my short life—in the shape of an old-fashioned Christmas tree, like a Currier and Ives Christmas card tree, framed by a snow-tinged window on a winter's night. Its enamel branches were laced with "snow," and semiprecious stones were scattered in abundance from top to bottom. The tip of the tree was crowned with a gold star with a crystal in the middle. To this day, I cannot think about that pin without feeling the love and security I felt as a young child, and realizing how fortunate I was to have someone who thought that I was special enough to merit this sparkling treasure. It was pure magic.

Through the years and the Christmas seasons to come, my prized Christmas tree pin was an annual adornment. I pinned it to college blazers, to the red wool cape that I had sewn myself, and to the first grown-up houndstooth suit I purchased to celebrate my appointment to a position by the California governor. I so treasured that pin and the memories it contained of Christmases past that I neither checked my coat nor let it out of my sight during its holiday forays.

In 1988 I attended my boss's Christmas party in the company of the love of my life, Kevin. Naturally I wore my Christmas pin. The combination of pink champagne and my frustration at our unresolved relationship brought the evening to an early and tearful close. I went home that night alone and unhappy.

As I sobbed alone in my house, I decide that if I immediately hung up my party dress and put away my holiday coat and purse, then perhaps I would have no physical memories of this night the following morning. It was as I was hanging up my black velvet duster that I noticed—the Christmas pin that had been with me for almost twenty years, for almost two thirds of my life, was gone.

I searched my car. It was not there. Frantic, I called my boss and asked him to look around his house. No, came the reply ten minutes later; it was not to be found at his house. Despite my broken heart and the 30-degree weather on that foggy night, I pulled a coat on over my flannel nightgown and drove the fifteen miles to my boss's house in my bunny slippers, armed with a flashlight and my prayers that the pin would be lying there on the sidewalk. I searched the surrounding neighborhood for forty-five minutes, but the pin was gone. And gone, too, were my cozy feelings of Christmas love.

The loss of that pin ushered in one of the darkest periods

of my life. The breast cancer that had ravaged my beautiful mother for almost ten years was now winning its evil campaign to take her life, and through rivers of tears and counseling I also realized that Kevin and I did not have the kind of future together that I both wanted and deserved. The prospect of those two losses occurring simultaneously in my life was unbearable. I found solace in myriad work projects, but I was scared to death. My father's grief at the approaching loss of his life partner, coupled with Kevin's emotional absence, left me alone to deal with my fears.

The Christmas of 1989 would be the last one we would spend with my mom. Through a miracle of God she was released from the hospital in time to attend Aunt Mary's traditional tamale dinner. I witnessed the joy in her eyes each moment she spent in the company of the family; I am truly grateful for my mom having had the strength to endure what would be her last Christmas season with us. She was storing up her own memories to reflect on during her quiet times in heaven.

My mother left this life just a few short months after that. Despite months of counseling before her death, nothing could have prepared me for the hopelessness I felt following her passing. There were entire days spent in my pajamas. I had lost half of my life base, and I did not know how to continue being the self-assured, ambitious young woman she had raised me to be.

But the darkness of winter passed and spring finally arrived, and with it the annual invitation to visit the beach house of Aunt Mary and Uncle Roger. My childhood was filled with summer memories of white sand, starfish, and walks with my parents on the beaches of Pajaro Dunes. The beach house was the last place I thought I could endure at this moment in my life. But my Aunt Mary began to wear down my objections. She was grieving, too, she pointed out, and returning to the very spot where we had enjoyed so many good times would be therapeutic for us all.

And so I agreed to go. Surprisingly, the drive itself offered peace of mind, and as the odometer registered the passing miles, my sense of tranquillity increased. Maybe Aunt Mary knew something that I didn't, something about facing our fears and healing.

At the beach house that year, Aunt Mary and I found common ground in the love and loss of my mom, her sister. We spent hours sitting on the beach, laughing and crying through our stories and recollections of summers past. On the last day of the trip, I awoke with a sense of rejuvenation. It had been so long since I'd had any energy that I assumed this burst I was feeling was due to the ocean air. I had no idea then that I had passed one of the most important tests of grieving, six months after losing Mom. I had returned to the scene of happy family times and faced painful memories.

The drive back to Sacramento began peacefully. I was in no hurry to get back, as I felt so serene and didn't want to jeopardize this newfound calm. Impulsively I stopped at a little town near Pajaro, a little town where the Main Street consisted of a block of antique shops. It was early morning, and some shops had not yet opened their doors.

The last antique shop on the right side of the street was open for business, though, and as I stepped in, I recognized the musty odor of old furniture and well-used books.

Through the maze of Victorian lamps and curio cabinets filled with silver spoons and other standard antique fare, I spotted the jewelry case in the back of the store. Perhaps there was some small trinket there that I could take away to remind me of my newfound strength.

I have always believed that things happen for a reason, and the sight that I then beheld affirmed my beliefs. There, tucked in a corner on an old piece of velvet, was the Christmas tree pin I had lost one year before. I asked the shopkeeper to remove it from the display case and, with trembling hands, turned the little pin over. Yes, this was it; the very same company name was inscribed on the back of the pin! In a miracle of rediscovery, I had found the one tangible thing I valued most, a treasure from my beloved past.

Though there was much work to be done emotionally for me and my family, I was now firmly on the way to healing. The boundlessness of the seashore, with waves breaking one after another for all eternity, and the Christmas pin that held within its branches so many feelings of warmth and love, were again returned to me. In the years to come, I would face other losses and disappointments, but I now knew that I possessed the strength and support from my circle of family and friends that would protect me and sustain my recovery whenever I needed them. And my holiday symbol of love, my Christmas pin, would again accompany me into another year of life.

—VALERIE J. REYNOSO
Sacramento, California

Christmas Doesn't Come
from a Store

*T*IME WAS RUNNING out. It was December 24—Christmas Eve—and I still hadn't found that magical feeling, the spirit of Christmas. I had done things I'd thought would bring it on—attended my children's school performance of Christmas carols, decorated our tree, baked, shopped, wrapped. Yet nothing seemed to spark the Christmas spirit within me. I had resigned myself to the fact that this just might not be a very good Christmas.

My husband, Steve, a firefighter, was on his routine twenty-four-hour shift at the firehouse, which meant he would not be home for either Christmas Eve or Christmas morning. Our four children and I were eager to spend what time we could with him, so we all drove down to the station.

As we arrived, the firefighters had just returned from a first-aid call to a nearby motel, where they had rendered care to a young boy with a fever and other symptoms. My husband expressed to us his feelings of concern and his desire to do something more for the boy and his brother and their mother. They had fled an abusive, alcoholic situation and were now hundreds of miles from home, with one change of clothes each, very little money, and now an ill child on Christmas Eve.

Steve looked at me and at each of our children and asked, "What else can we do to help them? We picked up a small tree on the way back to the station that we want to decorate for them, but what more can we do this late?" It was 9:25 P.M. Our children began a clamor of ideas. My daughter was sure a toy store somewhere was still open. I didn't share her hope, largely because even if we did find a store open, I didn't know how we would pay for anything we found.

I wanted to share as much as my children did, but this Christmas was already our leanest ever. Our own children were receiving only two gifts each. Still, we drove around eagerly looking for anything that might be open, planning to meet Steve and the other firefighters back at the motel room before the little family returned from the hospital, where they'd gone for medical care. Every store we saw was closed. Then one of my sons said, "Hey, I know somewhere that's open."

"Yeah, and they've got presents already wrapped!" declared the other one. Wondering what they were talking about, I pulled the car to the side of the street, and in frustration I turned to the kids and asked, "Oh yeah. Just where is this great place?" Their answer was so enthusiastic and genuine that it instantly ignited within me the flame of the Christmas spirit. "We can go to our house," they chimed together. "The presents are already wrapped and under the tree."

I asked them if they really wanted to do this, and their eager response was, "Yes. Yes! Now hurry!" Once we were home, I watched with wonder as they pulled name tags off of their presents and picked certain ornaments from our tree. At first, I was surprised to see that the ornaments they picked were the ones they themselves had made over the years. Then I realized that they were giving of themselves, and that these ornaments had special value.

Two of my boys came out of their bedroom with their baseball gloves, their "pride and joy" mitts. We loaded up the presents, some tree lights, and the candy and other goodies that served as our family's stocking stuffers, and then headed back to the motel. The manager let us into the austere little room, and we set right to work with the firefighters, who had also brought gifts.

We set the tree on the tabletop and adorned it with lights and the ornaments. Some of the firefighters hung candy bars and twenty-dollar bills on it with paper clips. Presents were placed under the tree, canned goods were stacked in the corner, and clothes for the mother and children were folded neatly on the nightstand. The room was transformed.

On each of the bed pillows lay a somewhat used baseball glove from our boys, and I saw my fifteen-year-old place between the mitts one of his most prized possessions. It was his home run baseball, which had been awarded to him after he had hit it in a home run. I doubted that the little boys receiving this prize could possibly know what a sacrifice this was or what a revered spot that ball had held in my son's room for the past six months. But that moment I knew that in my son's heart, the spirit of Christmas flamed brightly, lighting that little room even after we turned off all the lights except the diamondlike ones on the tree.

I had almost given up on finding that precious spirit of Christmas. But it was given to me by my dear husband, who recognized a need when he saw it, and by my children, who so eagerly responded. I realized as never before that the Christmas spirit comes to us most abundantly as we give ourselves to others.

—SANDI SCHUREMAN
Mesa, Arizona

An All-American Christmas

I T IS NOT often that we are given the chance in life to help another who really needs it. Because I lived in a comfortable suburban neighborhood surrounded for blocks in all directions by families that looked just like mine, the chances seemed remote that I would ever do anything that would have an impact on the future of a needy family. But I did, and it was truly a Christmas miracle.

I met Lupe through our parish priest at church. A single mother with six children ranging in age from six to seventeen, she had gone to the church to ask for suggestions on finding a job. Our priest knew that I ran a day care center at my home and was on the lookout for a full-time helper. He arranged a Saturday interview for her, and, recognizing a loving and kind woman who would work well with the children, I hired her.

We soon established a daily routine: She would find a ride to work, and at the end of the day I would drive her the short mile home. The contrast between the coziness of my house and the simplicity of hers was heartbreaking. Lupe lived with her children in a small house only minutes from my neighborhood, but her house contained only one mattress and a few chairs, since the winter before had been a rainy one and roof leaks had ruined most of the furniture and all of the other mattresses. Lupe and her children were sleeping on a concrete floor when I first met her. Through word of mouth and the help of some of my friends, we were able to find enough bedding for her children and a brand-new bed for her.

Over the months, I got to know Lupe very well. Although we did not speak the same language, I knew that she was a woman of pride, a very good mother who was willing to work hard to provide for her family. Her situation was not the stereotype of the lazy welfare family, so frequently portrayed in the press. Lupe was the sole supporter of the family that her husband had deserted. She had emigrated from Mexico with her husband more than a decade before and had obtained her citizenship in 1995, a fact of which she was very proud. Her children, however, were all considered illegal immigrants.

One winter day Lupe came to work very upset. When I learned the extent of her problems, I understood her emotional state. She had begun the complicated process of obtaining citizenship for her children, but after filling out the paperwork and paying application fees she had hit an enormous snag—since the children were considered illegal immigrants, she would have to pay a fine on each child before the citizenship process could be completed. The fine for each one of her six children was $650, a total of $3,900. And now that the process had begun and deadlines had been set, she could very well see her children deported to Mexico if she didn't pay the money.

I calmed Lupe down as best I could and called the immigration office to sort out what she was telling me. The situation was just as she'd described it—if she paid the fines, the children's applications for citizenship would go forward; if she didn't pay the fines, the children could be deported.

In addition to working during the week for me, Lupe and her children were already working weekends at the local farmer's market. There was literally no time left in the day in which to try to quickly earn more money. Bank loans were out of the question, as was the prospect of trying to borrow money from her other family members. I decided I needed to help this woman. I had grown to care a great deal about her and could not stand by and watch her family be dissolved.

I talked it over with my parents and my husband; we decided to try to raise the money for Lupe as a Christmas surprise. My father composed a letter that we could send out to family and friends. In the letter we described Lupe and her situation and asked for a ten-dollar donation. I gave copies of the letter to the parents of the children at my day care center and asked them to spread the word, too.

My first attempt at collecting money was with my weekly women's card group. They donated all of their winnings from that night and I came home with sixty-nine dollars. I was quite pleased with my first efforts at fund-raising and began to think that we just might be able to do this for Lupe after all.

I opened an account for The Children's Fund (as we named it) at my local bank and watched with pleasure as the money began to come in. In fairly short order we had received $1,200, almost a third of what we had set out to raise. A surprising setback arrived just as quickly, however: When the bank found out that The Children's Fund was for charitable purposes, they immediately closed my account. Stinging from this uncharitable act, I spent more than a week driving from bank to bank in an effort to find one that would take the money for Lupe's children. All this time I was getting checks in the mail every day. Even though we had only asked for $10 donations, I opened envelope after envelope containing $50, $200, or more. Neighbors were telling neighbors, my day care parents told their children's grandparents, and the whole effort snowballed.

The letters of support and goodwill that were folded around the checks were heartwarming. Many came from folks I did not know, and many of them told moving tales of their own immigrant forebears' arrival into the United States under somewhat less than legal circumstances. Despite the atmosphere of immigrant-bashing that reigned that election year in California, these strangers were opening their hearts and their wallets to an unknown Mexican woman. I knew that the holidays were a difficult time financially for many families, and yet here they were sending money to take care of the children of a stranger.

With Christmas only a week away, I was $850 short of the goal. The next day I received a check for $500 from a family who had decided to give all the Christmas money they'd received from their grandparents to Lupe and her children instead. A few smaller checks arrived to bring us closer to our goal, but we were still a bit shy of it. "A miracle," I told my next door neighbor, "that's what I need." And then the very next day, on Christmas Eve, one of my day care parents gave me a check for $200. In a little more than a month we'd raised the entire $3,900. The fines would be paid; the children could become U.S. citizens.

On Christmas Day my neighbor Gia invited Lupe, her children, and my whole family over for dinner. Some of the other neighbors and a few good friends joined us for the tearful moment when my husband and I presented her with a check for $3,900. Champagne flowed, and hugs were given freely.

There will soon be six proud new citizens of the United States. I will always remember the love, concern, and generosity of many people who helped this one family in need. Raising this money and seeing the look on Lupe's face and the happiness in her children's eyes meant more to me than any gift I have ever received. It truly is more blessed to give than to receive.

—CATHY CALDWELL
Rocklin, California

First Christmas

MY HUSBAND, MATT, and I had been married only two months, and our first Christmas together was approaching. It was also my first Christmas away from my family, which I knew would be difficult. I had always loved being with all my brothers and sisters during the holidays, and my mom had always made the season joyful with her traditional parties, wonderful cooking, and the excitement of dozens of beautifully wrapped gifts under the tree. She also had a special way of impressing on our family the deeper meaning behind our holiday celebrations, from the picture up on her bookshelf of Santa kneeling beside the Christ Child, to our Christmas Eve tradition of buying and secretly delivering gifts to a needy family. From her example, I have known since I was a young child that Christmas represents something very special.

And so, now that I was beginning my own little family, I wanted to create some of those same warm traditions and memories that reminded me of the real significance of the season, even if I was three thousand miles away from home. I had heard that my church, which puts on an outdoor living Nativity scene every year, was looking for volunteers to play the parts of Mary and Joseph. It was a tradition in the Washington, D.C., area where we lived, and I thought it would be wonderful to participate. So without even mentioning it to Matt, I signed up for both of us.

Matt is not a "performer," so to him the idea of being front and center stage as Joseph was a little unsettling. He had two main worries, he told me as we drove to the church that night: He was worried that he might have to say some lines during the enactment, and he was concerned that the church might not supply outdoor heaters!

When we pulled up to the church, we saw another couple who were just wrapping up their two-hour shift portraying Joseph and Mary. We were told that there was a ten-minute recorded tape that told the story, which repeated itself over and over. There was no speaking part for the volunteers, just a little bit of acting required. The baby Jesus was played by a "Baby Tender Love" doll, wrapped in old blankets—the same ones, I was sure, that were used year after year. Joseph would pretend to talk with the wise men while Mary held the baby doll and rocked it back and forth.

A gentle woman found us and directed us to the costume room. She picked out our robes and sashes and gave us our instructions. "When the recording starts," she said, "listen to the words and just go along with the story." Simple enough. We were to acknowledge the shepherds and the wise men when the time came, and devote the rest of the time to holding and adoring the baby. I figured that by the end of the two hours, on the twelfth time through the routine, we would have it down.

I came out of the dressing room with a blue cloak around me that was also draped over my hair. Matt was wearing a worn brown robe and, a tattered sash and had a fake beard glued to his face. I tried to hide my laughter when I looked at him, but we both knew how ridiculous we looked to each other. Matt still seemed somewhat uncomfortable with the idea of getting up on the stage, especially in his extremely fake-looking beard, knowing that many of his family and friends were coming by to see us. Because I had roped him into this "performance," I was feeling a little guilty. But we joked with each other as we walked out, determined to make the best of it.

As we approached the stage area, I was amazed at how many people were in attendance that night. There must have been 500 or 600 visitors before the night was through, and I suddenly felt a little stiff with stage fright. About the third time through the routine, I saw Matt's mother in the back of the crowd, waving her arms to get our attention. I was sure Matt saw her, too, because he couldn't keep the nervous smile off his face. Each time Matt and I exchanged glances, we both wanted to laugh, but we tried hard to focus our attention on talking to the wise men and fussing over the baby.

It was about the sixth time through the vignette before I realized how cold it was that night—only about 35 degrees. I pulled the blankets closer around the doll's little body and head, as any concerned mother would. I was gazing down at the baby, and the thought suddenly entered my mind: I wonder if it was cold *that* night—the night the *real* Christ Child was born? I began reflecting on the story I had heard so many times throughout my life and I tried to visualize the real Mary—not just as a character in a story written in words that were hard to understand, but as a person, a woman, a mother. Mary, the beautiful young virgin . . . a mere girl, really, several years younger than myself, who nevertheless would hold center stage in this dramatic event in history that would change the world forever.

For a brief moment, I felt as though I slipped away into another time and place. I saw the dusty stable and the rough dirt floor, a tiny wrinkled face against the straw. I could smell the musty odor of hay and cattle and saw the silent stabled animals, powerless to utter the sacredness they had witnessed. I looked over at my beloved husband, a simple carpenter, the only one who would hold my hand and wipe my brow . . . and give me an innkeeper's cool linen when the ordeal was over. And I saw the light streaming down from heaven, bursting through the slats of a crude stable, blending with the glow already radiating from a tiny, holy face. For that moment, I was no longer playing a part in a pageant. For one breathtaking moment, I *was* Mary, and I knew the tender emotions of her heart that wondrous night. As I embraced the baby against my chest, my heart swelled with a feeling I can only describe as pure love, and in that instant I knew that this child—God's own Son, the Savior of the world—also loved me. My eyes filled with tears of joy and gratitude for the warmth of His redeeming love.

Then I lowered my eyes to the crowd below and noticed a middle-aged woman who was standing alone, watching me closely, and she was weeping. Our eyes met, and then our souls touched, and we knew each other's thoughts. We were both reflecting on the woman Mary and what she must have been feeling that silent, holy night. Did she worry about the inadequate surroundings, or long to have the experienced hand of her own mother near during labor? Would she be prepared to raise this special child to fulfill his mission on earth, teaching him the tenderness and compassion he would need his entire life? When she looked into the smiling eyes of this new infant son, could she possibly know the pain and sorrow that would fill those eyes one day? Did she fear loving this child too much, knowing that her heart would break if he were ever taken away from her? Mary was the most "highly favored," chosen and blessed among women, but these were the concerns of a mother. Any mother.

As the woman and I looked deep into each other's hearts that night, we understood. Two people who had never met, and would never see each other again, had connected as women and as mothers—she, most likely a mother of children who had already left home, and me, a mother of a son to be born some months later.

I would never view Christmas quite the same way again. Although I would still enjoy the tinsel and wrapping, the decorated trees and the music, I would always remember that Christmas began with just a small family . . . far from home . . . and the love of a baby. I had felt for myself the real significance of Christmas. I knew my mother would be proud.

—KRISTEN GURKSNIS
Dallas, Texas

My Christmas Angel

O N A COLD and snowy December morning in 1971, as I waited in front of the Children's Hospital for two of my Montreal Expo teammates, I felt slight twinges of nervousness and even some fear about the experience I was about to have. As a father of three healthy, happy children, it had always been difficult for me to see little ones suffering severe illnesses and disabilities.

Just as I concluded a short prayer asking that we would be able to leave something of value with the children we were to visit, Steve Renko, a big, strong, right-handed pitcher, walked up with a look of concern on his face. He was feeling the same things I was. A few moments later we were joined by Boots Day, a usually happy, but very tough little outfielder. He also expressed how these visits pained him. This would be a bit different from our normal visits, in that we were to spend it seeing children in the birth-defects wing. I had visited many children throughout my years in professional baseball (it's what we *did*—it was the *least* we could do) most of whom had been stricken with various illnesses such as cancer and heart defects, and several of these children had caused me to offer prayers of gratitude for my health and that of my family.

As Steve, Boots, and I were entering the hospital, we were immediately met by the most cheerful nurse I had ever seen. She literally bounced toward us exclaiming, "Oh, we're so glad you're here today. We love our Expos!" I wondered how someone who spent every day around sick and dying children could be so bubbly. As she led us through the hallways, we could hardly keep up with her as she was telling us how excited the children were to see us. That made me feel grossly inadequate and overrated. Just because we could play baseball and were well-known in Montreal—did that make us special? I thought not.

Finally we came to a large room and as we entered, I prayed that the shock and sadness I felt did not show through my forced smile. What we saw were about thirty young children with twisted, deformed bodies, some terminally ill, some destined to live a life of almost total helplessness. I swallowed hard and followed our perky little nurse into the room.

Usually we would visit for a moment or two with each child, sign a picture or baseball card, and leave them with some mementos from the team. But this time we were ushered to the front of the room and introduced to the children. As we were walking up, I noticed that the room was full of Christmas decorations and commented to the nurse how beautiful they were. She said, "The children made them." When I said I couldn't believe it, she replied, "Well, we helped, but they did a great job." She showed me a painting of Santa Claus that a little girl had painted with her foot because she had been born without arms. I was close to tears when I saw that little girl beam with pride.

After we were introduced, the nurse said, "All right, children, let's show our guests how much we appreciate them." For the next fifteen minutes these little children sang Christmas carols to us in both French and English. I was now feeling the tears welling up to the point where I knew I couldn't control them. Here we had come to cheer these sick little children and instead, we were being lifted by them. It was a moment I will always treasure. While they were singing, I noticed one child with a head twice the normal size for a five- or six-year-old. The veins were straining at her skin and, quite honestly, it looked grotesque. She had a condition called hydrocephalus (commonly known as water on the brain) and I pitied her with all my heart.

When the music was finished and we had answered some questions from the children, we began to go from bed to bed and personally visit each one. Recorded music played "Hark, the Herald Angels Sing" and "Silent Night" as we did so. Most of the children were pretty cheerful despite their conditions, but when I came to the bed of the little girl with the enlarged head, she wasn't smiling. I autographed a picture for her and kept my eyes on it instead of her. Finally, as I handed it to her and said, "Here you are, sweetheart— thank you for the beautiful music," she broke into a huge smile and looked straight into my eyes with the most loving gaze I had ever seen. She touched my hand and asked shyly, "Could you give me a kiss good-bye?" Her voice was angelic. Her eyes held mine, and were the most beautiful clear blue I had ever seen. I bent down and softly kissed her cheek as she gently clasped my hand. What had so recently seemed repulsive to me had somehow been transformed into exquisite beauty. My heart now knew what it was to love someone unconditionally, and I felt that same love coming from her.

I had kissed an angel at Christmastime, and the softness and tenderness of the moment I shared with her comes back to me every Christmas, to remind me that no matter what we look like, or how we are shaped, or what our living conditions are, we can still give the ultimate gift to others. The gift of love transcends all material riches, and this sweet little angel had given that gift to me to keep forever.

As the three of us left the hospital that day and went out into the freezing air, ice formed on our cheeks where the tears still streamed—tears from three grown men who, because of the warm spirits of a few small children, would never be the same again.

Sometime later, I realized the thing I had learned most from those children was simply this: They were born with limitations, but through their short, difficult lives, they had learned to concentrate on what they *could* do instead of what they *could not*. And nobody had told them they could not be happy. I now knew why that nurse was so cheerful. She was able to share that incredible love and the children's amazing accomplishments every day. Living and working with angels like these would raise anyone's capacity to love.

Merry Christmas, my little angel, wherever you are. I love you.

—RON BRAND
Los Angeles, California

The Story of Punkin and Boo

HIS IS A Christmas fairy tale, with two good little girls and their sweet little kittens, helpful strangers, and even a miracle or two. But in fact it is not a fairy tale, as it all really did happen in Charlotte, North Carolina, in the winter of 1988.

My two young daughters, Lori and Ellen (who are very big now but who were then mere lasses of nine and eight) lived with their two kittens, Punkin and Boo, in our neat little house in the suburbs of Charlotte. The girls loved their kittens dearly and were hardly ever parted from them. Every night they tucked their kitties in bed next to them, singing lullabies to soothe their kitty nightmares and stroking them to keep their coats soft and shiny.

Like Lori and Ellen, Punkin and Boo were siblings, a brother and sister from the same neighborhood litter. Punkin (as you might imagine from his name) was orange, and Boo was a loving black kitten with a white dot on her nose, as though it had been dipped in sweet cream.

One day—on Thanksgiving Day, as a matter of fact—while our family was hard at work on the turkey dinner, the two kittens went out to play by themselves in the yard. They were well-behaved kittens so they didn't stray far, just over to the next yard to chase a squirrel or two or three. But those squirrels ran out into traffic, and foolishly, the kittens did, too.

Within the space of just a few minutes both kittens had been hit by cars. Thankfully, neither Lori nor Ellen saw this happen, but they learned the details later from some young boys playing basketball nearby who saw the whole scene unfold.

Punkin was hit first. The driver did not stop to check the kitty's condition, but just drove on toward his important business. Then Boo was hit. The driver who ran over Boo was also in too big of a hurry to stop and check on a tiny kitten as it lay in the street. That's when the miracles began.

As the boys told Lori and Ellen, although neither driver stopped for the kittens, other drivers pulled over right away. First a young woman stopped, picked up Punkin's limp body, put him in her car, and left. Then another stranger stopped for Boo. The boys didn't know where either driver took the cats, but they were pretty sure that of the two, Boo was certainly dead—the woman who stopped for Boo had had to pick her little body up with a shovel.

My husband Doug and I told Lori that Boo was dead. She cried for two days straight.

We launched a Christmas holiday search for Punkin, distributing flyers throughout the neighborhood and calling animal shelters to ask if he was there. When we came up empty-handed after searching all of the animal shelters in the area, we started to contact all of the veterinarians listed in the phone book. After several days of calling, we found him! He was somewhat battered and scarred, but otherwise in good health. The vet who had nursed him back to health wouldn't accept payment, and the Good Samaritan who loved animals enough to stop and pick Punkin up off the street and bring him in to the vet wouldn't accept the reward we offered.

And so from then on, Punkin would be the family cat, shared equally by the two girls now that Boo was gone. Lori and Ellen took turns sleeping with Punkin at night, but all three of them missed Boo.

What none of us knew was that of the two Good Samaritans who had stopped for our kitties on Thanksgiving Day, the second one was still working hard to bring Boo home.

I received a call one afternoon in mid-December from a woman who had seen one of the "Lost Kitty" flyers we had posted after the accident. "Thanks for calling," I said. "But we got our little orange kitty back. We found him at a vet's office." "Orange kitty?" the woman asked, sounding a bit confused. "No, I picked up a little black kitty in the street that day. She was pretty badly hurt but she is in better shape now. I've been trying to find her home for weeks, but I guess she's not yours. Sorry to have bothered you."

"A black kitty?" I asked quietly, not wanting to hope too much. "A black kitty with a little white spot on her nose?"

It was Boo! Boo with a shattered jaw, protruding shoulder, and mangled paw, but mighty happy to see us after all.

And so my fairy tale ends happily, with the good little girls and their sweet little kittens reunited by Christmas. My good little girls are in high school now, busy with homework and friends. But at Christmas every year I can still look into their bedrooms at night and remember the two little angels and their miracle kittens tucked into their warm beds, dreaming of sugarplums and catnip.

—MOLLY FURMAN
Charlotte, North Carolina

Exchange of Gifts

M Y HUSBAND, JOHN, and I had been blessed with three wonderful children and a happy life in the rolling hills of northern California. Throughout the early years of our marriage, I'd heard many stories about John's family, how they had come over to America many generations before, the impressive accomplishments of his forefathers, and wonderfully vivid tales of his own mother and father. It made for a rich family history. John took great pride in the book of Gallagher family history that his mother had written and published.

My own family story was not nearly as well documented. I knew a handful of colorful tales about my father, Wendell Thayer, and his rugged ranch life as a kid in a small eastern Oregon town, but he had died when I was fourteen. The tales had stopped, and I had long since lost track of that part of my family. Having three children of my own stirred up a sense that I should try to find out what I could about my family's history before the trail grew too cold. I didn't want my children to only know about one side of their family. As the year drew to a close and I geared up for my young family's Christmas, I resolved that I would spend time in the coming year trying to track down what I could. But where would I start?

Putting aside my thoughts of family roots, I threw myself into the Christmas celebrations. It is my favorite time of year. I love choosing just the right tree and hanging our family decorations. The house smells wonderful and I get that warm feeling of family, the advent of a truly blessed event, the continuity of generations, and the joy of remembering Christmases long ago.

My husband came home from the office one day in early December that year with a question for our youngest daughter: "Mary Beth, how would you like to fix up your old bike and give it to someone who could make good use of it?" Mary Beth had her eye on a new shiny yellow bike down at Dale's Schwinn Bike Shop. She was pretty sure that Santa would be dropping it off at her house Christmas morning, so she readily agreed to fix up her old purple bike to pass along to another child. One of the secretaries in my husband's office was divorced and having a rough time of it financially; her four-year-old daughter would be very happy to see Mary Beth's old bike under the tree that year.

But first, five years of bumps and bangs and rattles had to be smoothed away. Mary Beth and her dad cleaned up the bike with a little cleanser and polish. Then they took it down to the Schwinn shop and had it serviced. They tinkered and oiled and spruced up the works, and then added a new seat, tires, and handlebar grips with plastic streamers. When it came home, it looked like a brand-new bike, ready to make any four-year-old happy.

A few days later the little girl's mother came to our house to pick up the bike. That is always an awkward situation; neither party feels quite comfortable. The recipient of the gift feels a bit shy about having to accept charity, and the giver of the gift feels a bit shy about being so fortunate that they can give things away. It is an unbalanced relationship that all too often dims the joy of the moment.

I invited her in. We adults oohed and aahed over the newly restored bicycle and agreed that it would be perfect for her daughter. Mary Beth peeked around a corner and waved at the woman, too embarrassed to come out and join us. To smooth over the moment, I relied on that old conversational standby, "So, are you from around here?"

No, no, she wasn't from around Santa Rosa, California, she told us. She was from a tiny little town in eastern Oregon, she said, so small that no one ever knew where it was. "What town?" I asked, as my ears pricked up. "Vale," she replied. "It is way up near the border with Idaho." I knew exactly where Vale was, it was the same tiny ranch town that my father had grown up in, on the ranch that my grandfather homesteaded!

I knew the stories of dusty roundups and slippery calves, of chuck wagons and hearty ranch breakfasts, all from those faraway days when my father was still alive and from two hazy trips to see Grandma when I was still a small child. It seemed so far away, like a black-and-white movie I couldn't quite tune in.

And that is how things were until that day just before Christmas twenty years ago. This young woman not only knew about the Thayer family; she could describe the big old boxy house my grandparents built and tell me exactly where it was! It was painted two different colors—one floor was a dusty brown and the other a deep pea-green—and it was built on the banks of the Malheur River. With her help we were able to go back to eastern Oregon the following summer, find the Hope Ranch, and get in touch with what few relatives I had in the area.

I don't remember her name, but this woman gave me a lovely gift that Christmas. What started out that day as an awkward charity encounter had turned into a wonderful afternoon of mutual gift giving. She was able to give her daughter an almost new purple bicycle with a banana seat, and I was able to give my children a part of their family history they would otherwise never have known.

—WENDY THAYER GALLAGHER
Santa Rosa, California

The Riches of Family

Y FATHER, William King Driggs, was a classical music teacher, and during the Great Depression music lessons were a luxury very few people could afford, so we were very poor in those days as my father struggled to keep students. We actually weren't poor; we just didn't have any money. But we always maintained that we had everything money couldn't buy. Besides having musical talent, my dad was a fine artist and writer, so our home was filled with music, with his beautiful paintings, and with many books.

Dad had taught each of his eight children to play a different musical instrument. We traveled every summer with our little family orchestra, giving concerts at churches and schools throughout the West. We didn't have too much on the table to eat and certainly no goodies or snacks in the icebox, but somehow we always managed some flowers and candles on the table. Our parents saw to it that we enjoyed the romantic atmosphere of gracious living even if we had very few of the practical necessities. You might say that in some ways we were truly rich.

Of course, Christmas was a big time for our family. But I remember one year we were so poor, we had to cut down the pepper tree in our backyard because we couldn't afford to buy a Christmas tree. Mother had always managed to put away a few dollars toward the big holiday and produced miracles of her own to surprise us, but this year was especially difficult. All the childhood diseases had struck our family— mumps, chicken pox, measles, and even scarlet fever. The doctor bills took away any Christmas money there might have been.

We had a family council to see if we could find a solution to our dilemma. Mother came up with an idea that we all accepted immediately. She would make her delicious "divinity" candy, which she was famous for, and put it in pretty little boxes, and Dad would paint some lovely watercolor pictures and hand-frame them. Then we would drive out to some busy boulevard on a Sunday afternoon and try to entice the drivers to stop long enough to buy our homemade gifts. The spot we chose to set up our business was the corner of Los Feliz Boulevard and Western Avenue on the border of Los Angeles and Hollywood. We leaned signs against our old Dodge touring car and went to work. That area was the "Sunset Boulevard" of the day: Cecil B. DeMille, Jack Dempsey, and other celebrities lived in the elegant neighborhood. All the more reason for us children to hate the idea of standing out there "hawking our wares." Of course, we would have done almost anything to ensure a happy

Christmas, but the corner where we stood was very close to the city of Glendale where we lived, and I remember the agony of worrying that one of our friends might drive by and recognize us—even at the age of eight, I felt like I would die of embarrassment!

There was no magical ending to that episode. We stayed there all day in the southern California December heat— waving, flagging, yes, even singing songs and playing our instruments—and not *one* car or person stopped to buy one single item the entire day! We came home extremely discouraged, but still somehow managed to enjoy the beauty of the season, with the light from the candles on our little pepper tree and joyous Christmas music constantly filling our home.

That same Christmas remains clear to me because of another poignant memory. Each class in our elementary school had been assigned a needy family's name, and the children brought in canned goods and food items for a lovely basket for the family's Christmas dinner. I was as enthusiastic as the rest of the children about the project and contributed, too, although it was not easy to find anything in our pantry to spare.

A box was left on a classroom table for a couple of weeks for items to be deposited in, and I remember the feeling I'd get every time I noticed it getting fuller. I kept thinking of the family who might receive it—a family who would otherwise not have much of a Christmas dinner, who probably couldn't afford many presents or even a tree. During those weeks, I remember trying to visualize the family's reaction— their utter surprise and delight at the bounteous gift—and then their joy at being able to cook up a real "feast," with enough food to last a week! Because I was so consumed with the excitement of this little project, I gave very little thought to what I wanted for myself that Christmas. The true spirit of the season had created a warm feeling in my heart I hadn't experienced before.

The last day of school before Christmas I, along with a few other girls in my class, was asked to arrange the items in a huge basket and decorate it with a big bow and with some holly leaves and ornaments we had cut out of colored paper. That afternoon at home, just before supper, a lady came to our house and asked for my mother. When Mother came to the door, she beheld a beautiful basket of food, Christmas goodies, and even a turkey. As mother called all of us in to see the wonderful surprise, I immediately recognized every item in the basket, including my own decorations! My whole family was very touched by the anonymous gesture, but I burst into tears, devastated by the realization that some of my classmates would know that my family was the recipient of their charity. It was strange, but because of the intangible riches my family enjoyed, I had never considered myself poor, even though we really were—and suddenly the reality of our condition was very painful. That Christmas I had learned the lesson of the pure joy of giving, but I never dreamed I would also need to learn the important lesson of graciously receiving.

Year after year, Christmas after Christmas, our financial struggles continued, but my father refused to give up his dream of having a talented musical family of national fame. We lived out of a jelly jar full of the change that my parents brought home from the collection plate taken at the churches where we gave our little concerts. That jar was the only bank account we ever had. We seldom went to a dentist, had no insurance, lived in rented houses, and wore hand-me-down clothes throughout our childhood. My father felt he was a miserable failure most of his life because he hadn't given his children any real security.

Remarkably, however, at the age of eighty, that same man, handsome still and revered by his entire family, stood straight and tall, leading his children and grandchildren in the family's theme song, "Love at Home," on national television for all to see. His lifelong dream of that little family orchestra becoming something quite remarkable had come true at long last. The fifty members of the "King Family" (which had sprung from his original eight children) had performed at a charity event some months before, where the head of ABC-TV had seen them and asked them to do a pilot for TV. The show struck a chord in the heart of America, and the family went on to have a weekly show for several seasons. My father passed away shortly after one of the early shows, but he died "with his boots on," doing what he loved more than anything in the world.

My family spent the next decade doing television shows and concert tours. We have many wonderful memories of the experiences of those years. But I recall during one of our Christmas shows watching the entire family gather around a twenty-foot-tall Christmas tree on the set of the TV studio. It was decorated with hundreds of lights and elegant gold and silver ornaments. The women were all dressed in white satin and the men were in handsome black tuxedos as we began to sing "The First Noel." And in my mind I suddenly recalled another picture of a younger family, gathering to sing the same song, but dressed in much simpler clothing, around a much smaller tree—a pepper tree. The scene was different, but the blend of voices and the feeling of peace and love was the same. My family's humble beginnings were made beautiful by loving and wise parents who taught their children that Christmas and its true meaning and message is a miracle in itself. My parents, who felt that they had given us so little, had bestowed on us the most priceless gifts of life—music, beauty, and the security that comes from family love.

—DONNA KING CONKLING
Roseville, California

The Silver Star

I SHALL NEVER forget December 24, 1944, and the German prisoner of war who helped to make that night so memorable for me.

When the Allied forces made their big push into Germany, it was the duty of my military police battalion to take prisoners from the front lines into crudely constructed stockades. It was a bitter cold night and I found myself on duty helping to guard more than twelve hundred German prisoners. To say that the men in my battalion were a homesick bunch would be an understatement. The fact that it was Christmas Eve only added to our depression. One of our company, a man from the Smoky Mountains of Tennessee, stopped blowing on his hands long enough to say:

"What a cold, miserable Christmas! But just because we are stuck out here doesn't mean we can't do something about it. I'm going out to find a tree."

"Forget it!" another MP shouted. "There are no trees

around here. Besides, we haven't anything to decorate with anyway."

Not to be discouraged, Smoky went into the darkness and later returned with a bedraggled specimen.

"You call that thing a tree?" our heckler continued. "In Texas we'd plow that under for a bush."

With determination and a positive attitude, Smoky began to decorate his tree with ornaments made from gum wrappers, candy wrappers, any scraps he could find. Several of the men not stationed directly at the stockade began to help our zealous friend with his seemingly impossible task. As we worked, I suddenly heard a voice calling from the stockade: "American! American!"

Turning toward the compound, I saw a German prisoner with one hand extended through the barbed wire. With his other hand he was motioning toward me. I quickly threw a shell into the chamber of my rifle and approached him with caution. What I saw in his hand astounded me.

This prisoner had made a beautiful silver star, entirely from gum wrapper foil, that was a work of art. Each of the points was long and straight and its three-dimensional form made it glisten in the moonlight. He placed the star in my hand and motioned to the top of our tree. Hoping he spoke some English, I said, "This star has such detail, are you a professional artist?" By his puzzled expression it was obvious he spoke no more English than I spoke German, so I took his contribution over and placed it atop our tree.

"Well, I'll be!" my heckler began again. "I hate to admit this, but that bush is beginning to look like a real tree. Guess I should have kept my mouth shut, eh, Smoky?" A loud cheer of agreement resounded from all the men. As we completed our tree, we began singing Christmas carols, and I noticed several of the prisoners joining in on "Silent Night." The last strains were fading into the night when I heard the same voice call, "American."

This time the prisoner had both hands extended through the barbed wire. Again I approached with caution, rifle ready, and again I was amazed at what he held in his hands. This German sculptor had made intricate figures of the Nativity scene—Joseph, Mary, and the Christ Child. He pointed under our tree as he handed me his exquisite, detailed work. I nodded my thanks and carefully placed the delicate figures where he had indicated.

As I reverently arranged the tiny figures made of sticks artistically covered with foil, the light from our fire actually seemed to give them a heavenly glow. I contemplated for a moment, in our wretched, war-torn condition, how far we had strayed from the love of that first Christmas night, and felt tears sting my eyes.

Looking at the stockade, I saw the prisoner behind the barbed wire, gazing out at our humble Christmas offering. I hurried back, smiled, and warmly shook his hand. He returned my smile and the firelight caught the tears that were in his eyes.

Since the close of World War II, I have thought often of this German prisoner of war and the tender feelings I had for him that night. Our meeting was brief; we were two ships that passed in the night, but we shared emotions that crossed the barriers of language and the devastation of war. I have always wondered what happened to him but somehow I know that, no matter where he is, he would agree that our only hope for lasting peace in the world is a return to the teachings of the tiny figure he so beautifully molded that cold December night.

—IVAN T. ANDERSON
Kaysville, Utah

A Glimpse of Christmas

I T WAS ONLY several days until Christmas. My husband and I live in Venice, Italy, and we celebrate each day intimately, sweetly, with a thanksgiving that only people who have waited for each other seem to be able to sustain. We never wait for the calendar to drive our festivals. Still, it was my turn to program our Christmas journey—ten or twelve days to roam our beloved Umbrian hills, I thought. I sat in the *osteria* behind the ghetto, where I like to go sometimes to lunch on bread and soup, and to stay in the safety of old warm woods and soft light and the gentleness of the people who work and eat there.

The cook is named Giulia, and though she's lived thirty years in Venice, she wears still the imprint of the south, of her Calabrian blood and bones. She walks, generous flanks swinging easily, shoulders and neck brittle, carrying an invisible, ancestral water jug atop her head. At once an enchantress, an abbess, a goddess (who all do the same work, she says), Giulia believes in miracles. And on this particular afternoon, it was miracles about which she was convinced to talk. I'd come only for a bit of comfort and a place to think about my Christmas. She plunked down a liter-sized pitcher of Refosco, a fresh glass for me, one for herself, and I was fixed.

She opened by saying it is folly to ignore that myth and history and intelligence and hypothesis are inseparable, each being necessary to comprehend and embrace the others. There is great commodity in Giulia's security, able as she is to pull, willy-nilly, solutions, answers, from her stores of immutable truths. She is never bewildered. Nothing is illogical for Giulia except, perhaps, that one might seek to be free of pain. The only way, she says, to live without pain is to isolate, unloose one's self, so nothing will ever happen.

"A sort of blindness," I mused.

"Be careful," she said. "Don't confound the emotional death of a person with someone whose eyes don't work. I have a friend, Isabella, born in the village where I was born, who lives in Treviso. She has been blind for forty-six of her seventy-one years. She invites life in every moment, batting at it, willfully squeezing the joy and torment from it. She's the type who creates her own surprises. And she can see everything," Giulia said in her enchantress's voice. Inner sight, spiritual clarity, intensely heightened sensitivity—she spoke to these not uncommon traits of the blind, I thought.

"Yes, it's those," she conceded, "but also, on the past seven eves of Christmas, Isabella has been able to see, to open her eyes and see." I had no idea where we were heading. I poured more wine for myself. Giulia had yet to sip from her glass.

"The first time it happened," Giulia said, "Isabella was sitting, waiting for her daughter to come for her, to walk with her the twenty-five meters across the garden to the house where she lived. Together with her husband and their three adult children, they would share the traditional dinner of Christmas Eve there. She felt, heard, and then saw her daughter coming toward her—the daughter who was two when Isabella was blinded, the daughter who was then forty-eight years old. Was it illusion, a dream, a trick?"

Giulia continued to recount: "Isabella said nothing, touching her child's face and kissing her eyes as she did always. Her daughter felt the change. 'Mama, what is it? What's happened? Mama, Mama tell me,' she said."

"You are so beautiful," said Isabella to her daughter. Neither of them awake to anything but the moment, they walked to the other house, greeted the family, drank to their collective health and well-being. Isabella remained steady—no explosive announcements, no cries of sainted intervention. It was enough for her that it was happening. Isabella's granddaughter, daily companion to her since she was a baby, was then twenty-five, Isabella's own age the last time she was able to see. Isabella looked at her and saw the young woman who everyone had always said was in her image. She saw herself— herself as she had been—familiar, untouched, safe, as though time had neither thieved from nor redrawn her.

"Everyone seemed to understand, to accept," Giulia said, "that some sort of generous interlude was being shared by them." She said that no one—not Isabella, her daughter, or the children—doubted either that it was true or that it was ephemeral. No one raced to call a doctor or a priest. They were somehow prepared for it, anticipating it even as one might a shooting star, aware that its beauty was as precious as it was uncontainable.

No one expected that Isabella would wake the next morning still able to see. And she did not. The second and the third time on Christmas Eve that "the Graces came," as Giulia said in her abbess voice, the family began to think that some colloquy might be in order—some strike at understanding the event medically, physically. But Isabella was regularly examined, scrutinized by a team from the University at Padua. The physiological mechanism that permitted sight had been irretrievably destroyed. Still, the family brought their story to the university. The powers listened. Examinations, visiting doctors, probes, and theories were built and broken; there were no doubts that Isabella could not, would never, see.

Isabella continues to see. For a few hours, sometimes less, sometimes more, during the Vigilia, the celebration of the birth of Christ, Isabella sees. And no one who has ever known of these events has felt the need to sensationalize them or attach greater inferences to them. It's only that sometimes Isabella can see and that most of the time she cannot see. "Tranquillity with a thing so undecipherable is a gift of the southern mysticism," says Giulia. And we return to her comfort absolute in the face of the illogical.

"But what is she like—Isabella?" I ask of Giulia.

"She is tall and lovely with eyes unhaunted by their stillness," she says. "She lives with no fear. She laughs. She lives with no rage. She sees, tastes, smells, examines, caresses life as though it were ever on the edge of its moments. She is excited by music, by sun and rain, and the sound and smoke of her fire. She loves flowers and she loves bread. She eats cookies and drinks wine from the thin, etched goblets she drank from on her wedding day. She says memory is hunger. She says to live in the present is to be full.

"Her eyes are almost always full of tears, so much does she weep, does she ache for the beauty she feels and understands. *Sempre pieno di lacrime e briciole* [always full of tears and crumbs] is she, so that the first thing I do when I see her is to kiss the tears from her eyes and brush the crumbs from her breast," said Giulia in her goddess voice.

—MARLENA DE BLASI
Venice, Italy

The Good Samaritans

I SMILED HAPPILY to myself as I drove down the Colorado highway that afternoon, smiling in anticipation of seeing my family for a much-needed Christmas get-together. For two long years I'd been out of the country serving as a Peace Corps volunteer in Tonga, an island in the South Pacific, as one of the "Six Hundred Volunteers over Fifty," a program for older Americans. The scenery outside my car window was so different from the countryside I'd grown accustomed to; the dramatic snow-covered Rocky Mountains were a welcome sight.

My cheerfulness spilled over into friendliness toward my fellow mountain travelers—I had been playing "passing tag" with a U-Haul truck whose cab was filled with the excited faces of a father and his four young children on their way to a new home. We had become "freeway friends," smiling and waving at each other each time one of us pulled ahead.

It was their turn to lead as we came around the side of a

mountain. The U-Haul truck was ahead of me in the same lane when it suddenly began to swerve and slip in the gravel on the side of the road. I watched as, in what seemed like slow motion, the truck flipped onto its side and slid backward toward my car, then, still on its side, slid out across the highway, across the median, and into the fast lane of oncoming traffic.

I remember reacting very calmly, pulling my car off the road, carefully removing the keys from the ignition and placing them on my seat, and then walking across the now-slowing lanes of traffic to reach their truck. The next thing I recall is standing in front of the truck windshield, now topsy-turvy on its side with four children pasted against the windshield and fire and smoke shooting out the exposed bottom of the truck. The children and their father were trapped inside and shouting for help. I started to try to kick the windshield in with my heavy leather snow boot, but soon realized that would not work. Suddenly a car full of college boys stopped to help. One of them climbed up the side of the truck to try to yank open the passenger door and lift the family out. I ran back to my car for blankets. As I did so, a woman ran toward me, waving and shouting, "Get those boys off the truck; it's going to blow!"

By the time I returned with the blankets, several other carloads of folks had stopped to help and a hammer and a fire extinguisher had been found. Some wise person shouted through the window to the children and told them to turn their faces away while we shattered the windshield with the hammer. The children were handed down one by one into the arms of waiting strangers. Four women now sat on the ground, each hugging a sobbing child wrapped in a blanket. One of the highway Samaritans, an off-duty paramedic, ministered to the nasty bump on the youngest child's head.

It was close to forty minutes before the ambulance and rescue squad reached our mountain location, but by then things were under control and none of the children seemed badly hurt. I was struck by the way so many had stopped to help, but when I mentioned it to one of the college boys, he just shrugged and said, "That's what it's all about, helping others."

I returned to my car after the family left in the ambulance and continued my drive toward the ski resort. Still calm and collected about what had happened, I wasn't really overcome by the drama of the incident until later on that afternoon when I heard it reported on the radio news. Then I began to shake uncontrollably and wonder aloud, "Why wasn't anyone hurt? why wasn't the truck struck by oncoming traffic? why didn't the truck blow up when the boys were crawling on top of it and the children were trapped inside? why wasn't anyone hit by traffic when they stopped to help? why wasn't anyone thrown from the vehicle as it careened across the road?" It truly was a Christmas miracle.

Actually, there is a bit more to this story that I'd like to tell. During my entire Peace Corps experience I had lived in a country where for the first time in my life, because of my white skin, I was a minority. For two years I experienced nothing but kindess, love, and acceptance. During that afternoon drive in the mountains and my playful waving friendship with my "freeway friends," I had begun to reflect on the troubled turn that race relations in America seemed to have taken in my absence. My children had sent me letters overseas describing the O. J. Simspon trial and the great wedge that it seemed to be driving between blacks and whites. You see, the family in the U-Haul truck was African-American.

But the minute that truck crashed on the freeway, I can say with great pride, not a single one of those cars filled with people who stopped paid one bit of attention to the color of the skin of those they were helping. This was a family in danger who needed immediate help, and those who responded were happy to give it. As I drove away from the scene of the crash, I felt a renewed sense of faith that Christmas truly shows the inherent goodness and love of the ordinary American.

—SUSIE WAGNER
Denver, Colorado

The Sacrifice

*T*HE YEAR WAS 1932 and the nation's economy was at an all-time low. The disastrous crash of 1929 had left its mark, and we were experiencing a time that was to become known as the Great Depression. I was in the eighth grade, and we all started school that fall with few clothes and school supplies. There was no lunch program, and for many students there was no food to bring. So those of us who could bring something to eat shared whatever we had.

I remember that whenever any of us had an extra penny, we would put it in an envelope and hide it. When we had twenty pennies saved, we would take them to the store and buy two cans of Vienna sausages, a treat far better than candy. Then we would find a secluded area, put all our lunches together, open the cans of sausage, and divide everything equally. Those were special days.

As Christmas approached that year, we didn't feel the

excitement that usually comes with the holiday season. We understood about the Depression and knew there would be very little for any of us. But there was one desire we all had, though none of us would have mentioned it to our parents. A new sled had appeared on the market called the Flexible Flyer. With its sleek finish, sharp runners, and smooth handlebars that steered it easily and gracefully, it was the Rolls-Royce of all sleds.

We all marched to the hardware store one day after school to see the new wonder sled. "How much are the sleighs, Mr. Evans?" one of the boys asked.

"Well," he replied, "I think I can sell them for four dollars and ninety-eight cents." Our hearts sank. But that didn't stop us from dreaming the impossible dream.

School was finally dismissed for the holidays, and when Christmas Eve came, we had our usual Christmas play and party. We returned to our homes, happy, yet sad, feeling keenly the weight of those depressed times.

I awoke early Christmas morning but was not eager to get up. My mother finally called, so I dressed and we all went to the living room where the tree was. I was surprised to see that the tree had been redecorated and was more beautiful than ever. But the biggest surprise was still in store. There, underneath the tree, with a big red ribbon tied around it, was a shiny new sled—a Flexible Flyer!

I let out a startled cry and dropped to the floor, sliding my fingers along the satiny finish, moving the handlebars back and forth, and finally cradling the precious sled in my arms. Tears rolled down my cheeks as I looked up at my parents and asked, "Where did you get the money for it?"

My mother wiped away a tear with the corner of her apron and replied, "Surely you believe in Santa Claus. Open your other present."

I opened another box and there was a beautiful dress. I loved it, but my eyes were on the sled. I could only stand and gaze in awe. I was now the owner of a Flexible Flyer!

After our midday Christmas dinner, Mother announced, "Put on your boots and bundle up warm. We're going to town. We have another surprise for you." I didn't think anything could compare with the surprise I already had. Dad hitched up the team to our big sleigh, I loaded in my new sled, and we went to town. As soon as we crossed the bridge, I saw what the surprise was. Kids were everywhere, and so were Flexible Flyers. Main Street had been roped off so that we could start at the top of the hill and glide all the way down across the bridge without danger from cars. The entire community had turned out. Boys and girls were all jumping up and down, some were crying, most were throwing their arms around each other and shouting, "You got one, too!"

Our parents finally got us calmed down long enough to listen to instructions. Three farmers with their horses and sleighs would take turns pulling us to the top of the hill. The older boys went first, running and then flopping "belly first," as we called it, onto their sleds. We watched as they glided effortlessly over the crusted snow. Faster and faster they went, crossing the bridge and coming to rest amid the cheers and clapping of parents. We all took turns, and as the day wore on, we got braver and wilder. The boys discovered they could do tricks by dragging their feet in a certain way, causing their sleds to turn around and tip over. We all got caught up in this adventure, tumbling in a tangle of arms and legs, laughing helplessly as we slipped around, ending up in a pile of bundled bodies.

As night drew near, our parents called for us to stop—it was time to return home for chores. "No, no," we cried. "Please let us stay." Reluctantly they agreed, releasing us from chores for this one time only. When they returned it was dark, but the moon shone brightly, lighting the hill. The cold wind blew over our bodies; the stars seemed so brilliant and close, the hill dark and shadowy as we made our last run for the day. Cold and hungry, but happy, we loaded our Flexible Flyers and returned home with memories that would last a lifetime.

Everywhere I went in the days that followed, my Flexible Flyer went with me. One night I decided to go to the barn, as I often did, just to watch Dad at work. I noticed that one of the stalls was empty. "Where's Rosie?" I asked. "She isn't in her stall."

There was an awkward silence, and my dad finally replied, "We had to sell her. She cut her foot on the fence."

Sell Rosie? I thought. *Gentle, friendly Rosie?*

"But the cut would have healed," I said. "Why didn't you sell Meanie? She never does anything we want, but Rosie always leads the herd into the barn."

Dad didn't say anything, and suddenly I knew. Rosie had been sold to buy my Flexible Flyer. She was the best and would bring more money; and my parents had given the best they had—for me. I had always understood that my parents treasured me dearly, but until that moment I had never known a love so great. I ran from the barn in tears and hid myself behind the haystack.

I returned to the hill the next day and told my best friend about Rosie. "Yes, I know," she said. "My dad took ten bushels of apples from our cellar and took them to Pocatello and sold them door to door. He's never had to do that before. That's how I got my Flexible Flyer."

A growing amazement overtook me. "But how did they know?" I asked. "I didn't ask for a sled, so how did all the parents know we all wanted Flexible Flyers?"

Little by little we began to put the pieces together. Everyone had a similar story to tell. Then we began to realize how the entire community had united in one monumental effort of sharing, trading, peddling, extra working, and, most of all, caring, to buy the Flexible Flyers. None of us ever had the slightest hint of what was going on right under our noses. That had to be the best-kept secret of all time in so small a community.

When school resumed and we marched into our classroom and stood by our desks waiting for the teacher to say those familiar words, "You may be seated," it seemed we all stood just a bit taller. Not that we had grown in stature, but we had grown in a different way. Nothing had really changed. The economy was still the same and we still shared our lunches and saved our pennies for the sausages, but inside we had all changed. We were happier, we played harder, and we studied more diligently. It was as if we had all committed ourselves to be the best we could be, to make our parents and community proud of us. It was the only way we knew to say "thanks."

When the snow finally melted and it was time to store the sleds, we were reluctant to part with them. We clung to them as a child clings to a favorite blanket. They had given meaning to our lives and provided us with a sense of identity. That terrible monster, the Great Depression, no longer seemed such a threat to us. Somehow we knew there would be better times, a brighter tomorrow, and a more prosperous future.

Many years later, long after I married, I asked my mother how they had managed to keep that secret, and who started it. Her eyes twinkled. She gave me one of those warm, loving smiles that only a mother can give and replied, "My dear daughter, you must never stop believing in Santa Claus."

—ANEY B. CHATTERTON
Soda Springs, Idaho

A Miracle Touched My Life

ET ME TELL you about a miracle that touched my life. On Election Day, 1988, I was seriously injured in an automobile accident. I had been out on an early Christmas shopping expedition with my friend Joyce Petriello. As we approached a busy intersection on Highway 85, a speeding car knocked us seventy-five feet into the median. Luckily, we had our seat belts fastened. Joyce was not too badly hurt—her wrist was broken and she was bruised—but I was more seriously injured. As the rescue workers pulled me from the car, I told them my neck hurt. After X rays were taken, the doctors told me why my neck hurt so badly: Two cervical vertebrae had been injured, one of them so badly that my injury was classified as a broken neck.

My sons, Ennis and Wink, had heard of a fellow named Dr. Allen McDonald who specialized in spinal injuries. After looking at my medical records, he agreed to take me on as a patient. On November 14, I underwent a complex medical procedure in which bone was taken from my pelvis for use in a graft to fuse the injured vertebrae. This procedure was followed by the required surgical repairs on my neck. The doctors discovered that my spinal cord was not severed, but it was badly damaged. The prognosis was that I would live as a quadriplegic, completely paralyzed from the neck down.

Long after the surgery, I relived the long ride to the operating room. It was big and cold and bright with light, like something out of those old Buck Rogers movies. Then a deep religious feeling overwhelmed me: I was in the valley and shadow of death. God was my Shepherd, and I knew that it was only by His grace that I would live and would walk again some day.

On November 23 the doctor held a medical conference with me, my two sons, and their wives, Laurien and Bonnie. He gave us a devastating report: I would leave his spinal center in a wheelchair, I would require round-the-clock care, and I could never live alone. This was not what we wanted or expected to hear, but the family support was strong. My accident had humbled us all and drawn us closer to each other and closer to God.

As the news spread about the grim prognosis, relatives and friends everywhere started to pray for me. Members of their churches and members of my church in Fayetteville and even the church of my childhood in East Point all joined in prayer vigils for me. This kind of Christian loving care changed my attitude for the better; until then I wasn't sure that I wanted to continue to live helplessly paralyzed from the neck down.

I could raise my elbows slightly but could not lower them. I promised God that if He would help me, I would do every-thing that my medical team and physical therapists asked of me to the best of my ability. I promised God I would work hard.

I was the oldest patient at the hospital. Most of the pa-tients at Sheperd's Spinal Center were young people, eigh-teen to twenty-five years old. It was heartbreaking to see such fine young people condemned to helplessness.

To call a nurse I had to sip and puff and blow in a straw. To bathe me the nurses would put me into a fishnet stretched over a frame and hose me down. While I lay in bed, attendants turned me every two hours. I couldn't comb my hair, brush my teeth, or feed myself.

On the first of December, I wiggled my toes. My ability to move my toes was a sign of hope and the nurses and doctors all came to my room to congratulate me.

The week before Christmas my family came to the hos-pital and took special training on how to take care of me. My sons wanted me home for Christmas, even if only for a few days before returning to the hospital.

Just before my trip home for Christmas, there was a party at the hospital. The nurses wore reindeer costumes; the doc-tors wore Santa Claus suits. They all tried hard to create a holiday mood for the patients, but the party was a bitter-sweet experience. Some eighty patients in wheelchairs filled the room. I knew that few would be able to go home for Christmas like I would.

Yes, I did go home for Christmas that year. As my son carried me through the door into his house, he shouted,

"Here I come with my Christmas present for all the family!" On Christmas Eve I went with my family to church, despite my reluctance to face the world from a wheelchair. When we sang my favorite carol, "Silent Night," in the candlelit church, I was glad I had come after all. I felt close to God, and knew that I needed to strengthen my faith and trust in Him to help me walk again.

On Christmas Day, seated at the dinner table surrounded by the family I love, I was able to remove the leather straps that held utensils in my hands and eat without their aid. It was an incredible step in the right direction.

It was months later that I finally left the Sheperd's Spinal Center. On February 22, 1989, I stood alone with no cane and said good-bye to the staff and the other patients.

I praise God every day when I get out of bed and put my feet on the floor and walk. Not only did He hear my prayers, but He heard the prayers of all of the friends and relatives who prayed for me. Only one in a million quadriplegics is ever able to walk again, but I believe that I am a true testimony to the fact that God hears and heals when we pray and believe.

—MARIANNA SHUGART LANEY
Fayetteville, Georgia

Someone to Watch Over Me

I BELIEVE IN angels. Angels in heaven and angels on earth. I have been richly blessed to have three angels in my life, all of them men: my husband Michael, my priest Father Foley, and Fernie. Let me start with Michael.

In the summer of 1980, Michael and I were married by my lifelong friend and priest, Father Foley. Michael had a job with the Boulder Police Department, we soon had two sons, and life was good. We struggled to make ends meet as most young couples do; I had some medical bills due to a kidney problem, and we had the additional expense of Michael's flying lessons. Michael had grown up the son of an airline pilot, he had two brothers who were pilots, and flying just seemed to be in his blood. He continued his lessons for four years and finally became an instructor. All the money we had put into flying was going to be worth it someday when he got a job with the airlines.

Then in October 1990, the police came to my door one night to tell me that Michael had been killed in a plane crash. My world was shattered. For weeks, all I could do was cry. The hardest moment of my life was when I had to tell my two little boys, just two and four years old at the time, that Daddy wouldn't be coming home anymore. During those first months of overwhelming grief, my dear friend Father Foley would call weekly from Baltimore to check on me. I told him that Tommy and Ryan kept asking where heaven was and if they could go there to visit Daddy, and I said that I had no answers for them, only more tears. Father Foley gently offered a solution: "Tell them that Daddy went to heaven because Jesus needed someone to teach the new angels how to fly." It was, of course, the perfect answer, and it finally gave the boys peace. Father Foley also reminded me that all things happen for a reason, and that someday I would understand why Michael had died.

Our first Christmas without Michael was approaching and I was still numb. We had had company ever since the funeral, and someone from Michael's family or mine had been staying with us every day for the past six weeks to help with the boys and be of comfort to me. On top of everything else, there had been a recent homicide in our town and I was afraid of being alone.

A week or two before Christmas, my first night alone with the boys in our house, I received my miracle. I couldn't go to sleep that night—I felt so alone and so afraid. Tommy and Ryan had been sleeping with me ever since Michael died, and although the three of us were trying to pull together, the pain was still unbearable. That particular night

I was haunted by thoughts of Michael's death, wondering how long he had lived after the crash while the police searched for him in the mountains. I wondered where he was now—if he was okay—and if he missed us as much as we missed him. I guess I finally cried myself to sleep.

At about four in the morning something woke me up. I opened my eyes to a very bright light and saw a figure standing at the foot of my bed. The figure was brilliant beyond description and seemed almost transparent. Although the facial features were hard to distinguish, I immediately knew it was Michael. I sat up in bed and kept rubbing my eyes, thinking I was dreaming. But even more incredible than what I saw in front of me was the overpowering feeling of love—an inexpressible sweetness—that filled the room. Without words, the angel spoke to my heart, letting me know that he was okay, that he was in a wonderful place, and that we would be okay, too. He told me how much he loved us and that I shouldn't be afraid because he would be watching over us, protecting us. As I started to tell him how much we loved and missed him, my little Tommy woke up. He sat up in bed and pointed at the figure in front of us and said, "Mommy, is that my daddy? Yes, that's my daddy." Tommy and I hugged and cried and then very peacefully went back to sleep. I was no longer afraid to be alone. When Christmas came, I knew I had received a very special gift from God: the knowledge that Michael was watching over us and that we would all meet again someday.

The next few years were extremely difficult and at times I wondered if God had forgotten me. My beautiful mother, who had been my greatest support, died of cancer. My kidney condition was getting worse and I was told I would eventually need a transplant. And I needed help raising my two sons. I was only thirty-one and knew I would someday want to remarry if I could only find someone who would love my children as their own. Father Foley continued his support for me through those years, and always counseled me to pray to find such a companion, along with praying for a solution to my kidney problem. I followed his wise advice and prayed daily for those things.

I met Fernie at my bowling league. We were just friends at first, but after dating for about a year, I knew I loved him. He was wonderful to my boys, and together, we were able to start laughing again. We shared everything with each other—everything, that is, except my one secret: my need for a kidney transplant. I was getting sicker and sicker and I was afraid that if he knew the extent of my condition, he might not want to share in that burden—the cost, the months of recovery, the potential dangers. Two weeks after I finally got up the nerve to tell him, Fernie proposed to me. He wanted to share his life with me despite the hardships. I knew my prayers had been answered. Father Foley was there to marry us, and Tommy and Ryan, now five and seven, couldn't wait to start calling him "Daddy."

We hadn't even been married two years when I received the bad news: I needed a kidney transplant immediately. Although I was heartsick, the doctors told me that between my five brothers and sisters, I should be able to find a donor who would match my blood and tissue type. My blood was A positive and anyone with type A or O could be a possible match, provided they had the same tissue type. My wonderful brother Dave told me he'd give me *two* kidneys if I needed them, but when he went down to be tested, found out his blood was B positive. As it turned out, all my siblings had the wrong blood type except one brother, who unfortunately had only one kidney.

Fernie knew how upset and afraid I was, and with great tenderness said, "Honey, I have A positive blood—I'll give you a kidney." We both knew the odds of his tissue being a match and lightly dismissed the thought, until I went to the hospital for tests. When they asked me if I had a donor and I jokingly told them my husband was willing, they decided to test him. Our blood was mixed together to see if there was any rejection factor, and amazingly, we were a perfect match—blood *and* tissue type. My husband, my hero, was willing to go through this extremely dangerous and painful procedure to make me whole again. Somehow I knew God and Michael were still up there together working miracles for me, and they had sent me Fernie.

Of the 665 kidney transplants performed at Presbyterian St. Luke's Hospital, none had been done between a husband and wife. It simply doesn't happen. Ours was their first, and it was a complete success. We were released in less than a week, and six weeks later, we enjoyed the best Christmas ever. We were a family now, healthy and happy, blessed by many miracles. I had believed our angel when, a few Christmases before, he had so lovingly assured us we would be okay, but I never dreamed that the two greatest desires of my heart would be provided by one remarkable man. I will be forever grateful, and I will continue to watch for angels.

—DIANNE CAMPBELL-OSTDIEK
Lafayette, Colorado

We would love to hear about
your Christmas miracle.
Please send your story to:

JENNIFER BASYE SANDER
BIG CITY BOOKS
P.O. BOX 2463
GRANITE BAY, CALIFORNIA
95746-2463

Please include your address and phone
number so we can contact you.

Acknowledgments

OUR WARMEST THANKS to the *real* "miracle workers" at William Morrow, especially Senior Editor Toni Sciarra and Assistant Editor Katharine Cluverius, and our extraordinary agent, Sheree Bykofsky.

Our deep gratitude to all of the following people: Bill Adler, Jr., Xan Albright, Jettie Jacob and Ivan T. Anderson, Barbara Arfsten, Scott and Lindsey Arfsten, Kerstin Backman, the Basye family, George Bingham, Ross and Diane Bjella, Marlena de Blasi, Daryl Bohnstedt, Ron and Candy Brand, Lori Buher, Yvonne and Bill Burch, Katherine Burns, Anne Burt, Margaret Cable, Cathy Caldwell, Dianne Campbell-Ostdiek, Aney B. Chatterton, Jane Clayson, Chris Conkling, Jim and Donna Conkling, Brooke Cowan, Delys Waite Cowles, Chuck and Barbara Curtis, Holly DeGroot, Virginia Dolar, Ben and Nancy Dominitz, John Emery, Diana Griego Erwin, Pete and Joan Fellows, Molly Furman and the Furman family, Wendy Thayer Gallagher, Jannis Gard-

Acknowledgments

ner, Kit Dillon Givas, Stanley Glassover and the rest of the Glassover family, Dr. Bruce Goldberg, Linda Grimes, Gayle Groberg, Vivian Gundestrup, Kristen Gurksnis, Mark Victor Hansen, Pat Huber, Inez Humphries, Rabbi Abie Ingber, Mary Kelly, Sally Kuch, Rahima Kupper, Marianna Shugart Laney, Miki Hsu Leavey, Pete Lewis, Nora Lynn, MarGene B. Lyon, Raynier Maharaj, Gary McCann, Isaiah McKinnon, Elisabeth McPhail, Frank G. Miller, Michael Miller, Sherry Miller, Vicki Mitchell, Allyson Moring, Robin Montgomery, Karen Morrow, Tonya Morrow, Laura Mulrooney, the Northam family, Cathe Odom, Sabine Painter, Dr. Helen Pensanti, Jenn Pfeiffer, Olivia Pratt, Louise Reardon, *Reader's Digest*, Carla Rey, Valerie J. Reynoso, Mary Jane Rhodes, Mary Beth Gallagher Salmon, Peter Sander, Rev. Howard C. Schade, Sandi Schureman, Beverly Shaver, Cynthia Stewart-Copier, Cathleen Swanson, Jeanne Tate, Kelly Strong Thacker, Jan Tilmon, Christopher J. Trujillo, Nancy Trythall, Susie Wagner, Marian Jeppson Walker, Teresa Walker, Laurette Walton, Todd Walton, Bonnie Williamson, and Velora Wells.